DISCOVERING PORTUGUESE

A BBC Television course in Portuguese for beginners

by

Alan Freeland

Lecturer in Portuguese and Spanish,
University of Southampton

Edited by
Terry Doyle

BBC BOOKS

Discovering Portuguese, a BBC Television course for beginners, was first broadcast from May 1987. The series was produced by Terry Doyle.

It consists of:
6 television programmes
1 course book
A set of 2 audio cassettes

Published to accompany a series of programmes prepared in consultation with the BBC Continuing Education Advisory Council.

Picture Credits
Acknowledgement is due to the following for permission to reproduce photographs:
BARNABY'S PICTURE LIBRARY pages 43, 45 *left,* 46, 104 *top,* 138 & 146; CALOUSTE GULBENKIAN FOUNDATION, LISBON pages 121 & 149; CAMERA PRESS page 125; J. ALLAN CASH PHOTOLIBRARY pages 18, 62, 67, 69 *left* & 105; TERRY DOYLE pages 15 *top,* 35 *top,* 54, 55, 70 *bottom,* 76, 87, 88, 106 *both,* 120 & 129; ROBERTA FOX pages 69 *right,* 81 *both,* 82, 86 *both* & 104 *bottom;* PHOTO SOURCE page 83; PICTUREPOINT, LONDON page 35 *bottom;* PORTUGUESE NATIONAL TOURIST OFFICE pages 25 *bottom,* 44, 45 *right,* 64 & 122; SPECTRUM COLOUR LIBRARY page 25 *top* & *centre;* TOPHAM PICTURE LIBRARY page 70 *top;* PAUL C. WALDOCK pages 15 *bottom,* 29 & 33.

The cover pictures were taken by Roberta Fox and Terry Doyle.

First published 1987
Published by BBC Books, a division of BBC Enterprises Limited
Woodlands
80 Wood Lane
London W12 0TT
ISBN 0 563 21345 0

Designed by José Brandão, Lisbon
Cover design by Rachel Hardman
This book is set in Garamond, and printed and bound in Portugal by Novotipo, Lisbon

Contents

Acknowledgements

Many people in both Portugal and the UK have contributed to this course in various ways. I would particularly like to thank the following: my wife Jane Freeland (School of Languages and Area Studies, Portsmouth Polytechnic) for her invaluable help in designing the syllabus; Terry Doyle of BBC Continuing Education Television for his constructive advice on linking the various components of the course and for his enthusiastic collaboration at every stage; my colleagues in Portuguese Studies at the University of Southampton for their useful comments on the typescript, especially Maria da Conceição Silva for her generous and expert assistance; Maria-Elena Schambil for her very helpful contributions on Brazilian Portuguese; Elizabeth McDowell and Roberta Fox for their hard work relating to the cassettes; Jennie Allen and Frank Holland of BBC Books for their efficient management of the production of the book; John Pride for his patient assistance in checking the typescript and proofs; and José Brandão for his excellent work as designer; finally, my son Daniel for his guidance on how to use a computer to achieve alphabetical order in the Glossary!

Alan Freeland
Department of Spanish, Portuguese and Latin American Studies,
University of Southampton

Introduction

Discovering Portuguese is a course for the beginner who wants
to develop basic skills in speaking and understanding the language.
Throughout the course, you are encouraged to notice how Portuguese
works, so that you can gradually progress from being taught to
becoming an independent learner, able to extend your skills further
by listening to people and by reading. In addition, since language is
inseparable from the way of life and the culture of those who speak it,
Discovering Portuguese is also an introduction to Portugal and its
people.

Portuguese, of course, is more than the language of Portugal. In terms
of the numbers of speakers, it ranks fifth in the world — after Chinese,
English, Russian and Spanish. This position is due mainly to Brazil,
Angola and Moçambique, to mention only the largest Portuguese-
speaking areas. In this course you will learn the Portuguese of Portugal
— *o português de Portugal* — but you will not have difficulty in adapting
this to the varieties spoken in other parts of the world.

The course

The course consists of six BBC television programmes, this book and
two sound cassettes. The book and cassettes are closely integrated, but
are designed to be used independently of the television programmes.
You can use the course either to work on your own or, better still, since
language is for communicating, with another learner or in a class.

The book and cassettes are divided into two parts. **Part I** consists of six
units which follow the television programmes, expanding considerably
on what is taught in them and providing opportunities for you to
practise and to check that you are producing understandable
Portuguese. Each unit introduces a sequence of dialogues, specially
recorded for this part of the course. The dialogues are used to show
you how to deal with particular situations, such as ordering a meal
or asking the way. But while you are practising language in specific
situations, you are also learning skills which you can use in a wide
variety of other situations — more about this feature of the course in
a moment. In addition to the language material, and usually closely
related to it, each unit contains pieces in English about Portugal and
the Portuguese, which form an introduction to the country and people.

Part II consists of an anthology, a reference grammar, a key to the
exercises and a glossary. There is also a note on pronunciation and a
brief guide to some of the differences in vocabulary and pronunciation
between European and Brazilian Portuguese.

The anthology is a series of extracts from interviews recorded in Portugal during the filming of the television series. If you have the opportunity to watch the television programmes, some of this material will be familiar. The interviews on the cassette are accompanied in the book by notes on language, by transcripts of what is said and by English translations.

Suggestions on using the course

Part I

The book and the cassettes should be used together, because the sound of Portuguese, like English if it isn't your native language, takes some time to get used to. So it's essential to have plenty of opportunities to listen to it. Many of the activities in the book require you to listen, participate and then check what you have been doing by further listening or by consulting the Key.

The book gives you the text of the dialogues recorded on the audio cassettes (except in a very few cases where there is a particular reason for listening only). Material recorded on the cassettes is indicated by a symbol (see left). In some of the exercises, where you are asked to take part in a dialogue, you may find it helpful to read the text in advance and rehearse what you are going to say. But, apart from such exercises, we recommend you to listen to the dialogue on your cassette, more than once if necessary, before you read. Don't worry if you can't understand it all — the important thing is to get the gist of what is being said. Of course, it's easier to read the words first and then listen, and from time to time you may need to do this. But in the end you will want to understand spoken Portuguese without seeing it written down, so you should work at your own pace towards this goal.

At the end of each sequence of dialogues, the most important points about them are summarised in a box. You need to be familiar with the contents of each box as you work through the course as they gradually build up into skills you can apply in different situations. There is a summary of these skills at the end of each unit, set out so that you can see immediately how to use them in new ways, simply by 'slotting in' other words from elsewhere in the book or from a dictionary.

At the end of each unit there is also a list of what we consider the most useful vocabulary that has cropped up in the dialogues. These lists are to enable you to check that you know the meanings, so only the Portuguese is given. If you find you have forgotten what a particular word means, turn back to where it is used or consult the glossary at the end of the book.

Although the course lays particular stress on understanding spoken Portuguese and on speaking it yourself, Part I also includes some written exercises and suggests further ways to practise writing. In fact, many of the exercises could be done in writing and checked in the Key. However, we suggest you always speak your answer first and then, if you wish, try writing it.

Part II

The anthology of interviews can be used in a variety of ways. You can simply read the English introductions and the translations as a selection of personal viewpoints on Portugal that relate to themes in the television programmes and in the first part of the book.

Or you can use it to help you go beyond what you have learned in Part I and get used to discovering more Portuguese for yourself through reading and listening to people. We don't expect you to be able to understand the interviews straight away. So, to use them fully, you will need to do a certain amount of work on them, and suggestions on how to set about this are made at the beginning of Part II.

The Grammar provides a brief summary, for reference purposes, of the language contained in Part I. However, it is perfectly possible to complete the first part of the course without taking up the occasional invitations to refer to the Grammar. The Grammar is also designed to expand the possibilities of the course. You can use it, together with the material in the anthology, to help you launch out into the Portuguese-speaking world.

Finally, a word of advice if you are learning on your own. You will probably find it more effective to use the course for half an hour a day than to attempt a long session at intervals of several days; so deal with part of a unit at a time. You will also find it necessary occasionally to revise a unit, or part of a unit, that you have covered earlier. A little, often, and constant revision are the keys to what we hope you'll find both an enjoyable and an effective voyage of discovery. *Boa viagem!*

ESPANHA

BRAGANÇA

VIANA DO
CASTELO

MINHO

BRAGA

TRÁS-OS-MONTES

VILA REAL

PORTO

DOURO

BEIRA ALTA

VISEU

AVEIRO

GUARDA

OCEANO

ATLÂNTICO

COIMBRA

BEIRA LITORAL

BEIRA BAIXA

LEIRIA

PORTALEGRE

ESPANHA

SANTARÉM

ESTREMADURA

RIBATEJO

ALTO ALENTEJO

LISBOA

ÉVORA

SETÚBAL

BEJA

*Map of mainland
Portugal
showing
traditional
regions
and major
towns and
cities*

BAIXO ALENTEJO

ALGARVE

FARO

OCEANO ATLÂNTICO

Part I

1 FAZ FAVOR

In this first unit you'll learn how to greet people, how to ask for things in a simple way, and how to ask certain kinds of questions. The unit also deals with some features of Portuguese which make it sound very different from English.

Greeting people

1   Listen to the first three items on your cassette. Various people are greeting each other at different times of day, and asking each other's name.

Ana	Bom dia.
João	Bom dia.
Ana	Como é que se chama?
João	Chamo-me João. E você?
Ana	Eu chamo-me Ana.

Bom dia   *Good morning*
Como é que se chama?   *What is your name?*
(Eu) chamo-me...   *My name is...*
E você?   *And you?*

Pedro	Boa tarde.
Manuel	Boa tarde.
Pedro	Como é que se chama?
Manuel	Chamo-me Manuel. E você?
Pedro	Eu chamo-me Pedro.

Boa tarde { *Good afternoon*
            Good evening

José	Boa noite.
Alice	Boa noite.
José	Como é que se chama?
Alice	Chamo-me Alice. E você?
José	Eu chamo-me José.

Boa noite { *Good evening*
            Good night

The appropriate greeting depends on the time of day:

bom dia   in the morning until lunch-time
boa tarde   in the afternoon until it gets dark
boa noite   from nightfall onwards

You can use the same expressions when taking leave of someone at different times of day.

> To ask someone's name: **Como é que se chama?**
> Or, more simply: **Como se chama?**
>
> To tell someone your name, begin: **Chamo-me...**
> and add your name.
>
> The **ch** in Portuguese is pronounced the same as **sh** in English
> (e.g. 'shall').

2 Rewind your cassette and listen to items 1-3 again. This time, press the
pause button after each phrase and repeat the phrase yourself. Try this
without reading the words off the page. Concentrate on imitating the
rhythm of the phrase and trying to stress the right syllable.

Sounds Portuguese

A striking feature of Portuguese is its nasal sounds. You may have
noticed a nasal sound in **bom dia** and some of the other phrases you
have heard.

Listen to the nasal sound in the following words. These will crop up
shortly in dialogues.

com	*(with)*	**donde**	*(from where)*
sem	*(without)*	**Londres**	*(London)*
sim	*(yes)*	**inglês**	*(English)*
não	*(no)*	**muito**	*(very, much)*

> The nasal sound occurs:
>
> in vowels that have the written accent ~ above them (known in
> Portuguese as the **til**): **João, não,** etc.
>
> when a word ends in **m** or **ns**: **bom, sim,** etc.
>
> when a vowel is followed by **m** + a consonant, or by **n** + a
> consonant: **Edimburgo, Londres,** etc.

A special case is the word **muito,** which sounds almost as though it
were written 'muinto'.

Rewind your cassette and practise the examples. Notice that if the
syllable or word ends in **m**, the **m** is not pronounced. That is, you
don't close your lips after the nasal vowel.

If you think of the **til** as indicating a 'missing' **n**, you will sometimes be
able to make sense of the word in which it occurs. For example, **limão**
(lemon), **João** (John). It's also useful to notice that the **-ão** ending often
corresponds to the English ending -ion: **televisão, missão.**

The nasal sound hardly exists in English, but if you speak some French
you will be familiar with it. Some English-speakers pick it up fairly
quickly, others have great difficulty. You will be understood even if
your nasal vowels aren't perfect!

4 People are asking each other their names and where they are from. Try to work out who is from where. Use the map to help you, then check your answers in the Key. (A few cities have Portuguese names.)

> **Donde é?** *Where are you from?*
> **Sou** *I am*
> **Sou de…** *I'm from…*

Now say which town or city you are from.

1 Inglaterra · Londres
2 Escócia · Edimburgo
3 Gales · Cardife
4 Irlanda · Dublim

Sounds Portuguese

5 You may have noticed that an **s** at the beginning of a word — for example in **sou** — sounds like the **s** at the beginning of a word in English, as in 'some'.

You may also have noticed a **sh** sound in some of the language you have heard, like the beginning of 'shall' in English. This sound occurs when a written word ends in **s** or **z,** or when an **s** is followed by certain consonants (**c, f, p** or **t**).

Listen to the following words on your cassette and practise them.

português	galês
inglês	faz favor *(please)*
escocês	pastel *(a pastry)*
irlandês	nescafé

One further point about the pronunciation of **s.** When it occurs between two vowels, it represents a sound like the **z** in 'zoo'. Listen again to your cassette and repeat the examples.

portuguesa	irlandesa	escocesa
galesa	inglesa	

These are the 'feminine' forms of several words for nationality. ('Masculine' and 'feminine' forms will be explained later.) To make sure you have grasped the difference between the **sh** and **z** sounds, listen again to your cassette and try saying both the masculine and feminine words for these nationalities.

português portuguesa	escocês escocesa	inglês inglesa
galês galesa	irlandês irlandesa	

6 In the process of practising your pronunciation you have learned enough Portuguese to introduce yourself in a simple way. Try saying what nationality you are, and where you are from. For example, if you were a man from Lisbon, you might say: **Sou português. Sou de Lisboa.** Or, if you were a woman from Lisbon: **Sou portuguesa. Sou de Lisboa.** If necessary, use a dictionary to find the Portuguese word for your nationality.

The next item on your cassette gives you one side of a dialogue. Someone greets you, asks your name and then asks where you are from. Use the pauses to reply, and as well as saying where you are from say what your nationality is. If you find the pauses too short, use your pause button.

O Café

7 **Café** means both 'café' and 'coffee', and both are important to the Portuguese. Much more than in English-speaking countries, the café is a centre of social life — a place to meet friends, to watch the world go by, or to read one of the many daily newspapers.

Closely related to the café is the **pastelaria** — a café that specialises in cakes and pastries. The Portuguese have a sweet tooth, and an enormous inventive genius goes into the preparation and presentation of all that you will find on display in the best **pastelarias.**

An indication of the importance of coffee for the Portuguese is the number of words for it. Where English distinguishes mainly between black coffee and white coffee, Portuguese has several words, including some regional terms. The different words indicate whether the coffee is small or large, strong or weak, with or without varying quantities of milk. If you ask for **um café** you will either be served **uma bica** or asked if that is what you want — a small, very strong, black coffee. **Um garoto** is a small white coffee, **uma meia de leite** is a larger white coffee (tea-cup size). Or you could have **um carioca,** a weaker black coffee, or **um galão,** coffee served in a glass with a lot of milk. The most useful words to begin with are **uma bica** and **um garoto.**

If you don't drink coffee, you could have **um chá.** This is the same word for tea as in Cockney English, but pronounced differently, and is originally derived from Mandarin Chinese. The Portuguese were the first European voyagers to the East — but more of that later.

15

Normally, if you ask for **um chá**, it will be served **sem leite** (without milk). So if you want milk, ask for **um chá com leite. Um chá com limão** is tea with a slice of lemon. **Um chá de limão** is a deliciously refreshing infusion of lemon — 'lemon tea'.

Ordering

8   A customer calls the waiter and orders a small white coffee. 'The customer' is **o cliente**. 'The waiter' is **o empregado**. Notice, however, that you do NOT attract the waiter's attention by calling **'Empregado!'**

Cliente	Faz favor!
Empregado	Que deseja?
Cliente	Um garoto, se faz favor.

The waiter brings the coffee...

Cliente	Quanto é?
Empregado	São 30$00.
	Customer pays...
Empregado	Muito obrigado.

To order something, name it and add: **se faz favor**

To attract the waiter's attention: **Faz favor!**

Faz favor
Se faz favor } *Please*

(If you are a man)		(If you are a woman)
Obrigado } *Thank you*		**Obrigada**
Muito obrigado } *Thank you very much*		**Muito obrigada**

Que deseja? *What would you like?*

Quanto é? *How much is it?*

---

9   Carlos and Teresa order drinks, including lemon tea and black coffee, and something to eat. Which of them asks for black coffee?
(See **Key** for answer.)

Empregado	Boa tarde. Que desejam?
Teresa	Um chá de limão e um pastel de nata, se faz favor.
Carlos	Uma bica e uma água mineral sem gás.
Empregado	Fresca ou natural?
Carlos	Fresca.
Empregado	Mais alguma coisa?
Teresa	Mais nada, obrigada.

um pastel de nata   *a kind of custard pastry*
água mineral   *mineral water*
sem gás   *still*
com gás   *fizzy*
fresca ou natural   *cool or normal (i.e. room) temperature*

> **Que desejam?** *What would you like?* (addressed to more than one person)
>
> **Mais alguma coisa?** *Anything else?*
> **Mais nada** *Nothing else*
>
> **com** *with*
> **sem** *without*
> **e** *and*

10 Domingos and Helena fancy an afternoon snack, **um lanche** – a word imported from English 'lunch', but with a different meaning. **Lanchar** is to have an afternoon snack. This might include **uma sanduíche,** another word that has come from English (a sandwich).

Listen now to your cassette. Is it Domingos or Helena who orders coffee? (See **Key** for answer.)

Domingos	Faz favor!
Empregado	Boa tarde. Que desejam?
Domingos	Uma cerveja e uma sanduíche de fiambre, faz favor.
Helena	Um galão e uma torrada com manteiga.
Empregado	Mais alguma coisa?
Helena	E um copo de água, se faz favor.

uma cerveja *a beer*
uma sanduíche de fiambre *a ham sandwich*
uma torrada *a (double) slice of toast*
manteiga *butter*
um copo *a glass*

11 You will have noticed that the word for 'a' is sometimes **um** and sometimes **uma**. Which you use depends on whether the word that follows is 'masculine' or 'feminine', shown in dictionaries by the abbreviations **m.** and **f.**

Similarly there are two words for 'the': **o** (m.) and **a** (f.)

m.	f.
o leite	a bica
o limão	a pastelaria
um café	uma sanduíche
um pastel	uma cerveja

As you come across new words, learn them together with the appropriate word for 'a' or 'the'. Further guidance on masculine and feminine is given in **Grammar 1** and **5.1**.

Something to try with a beer in Portugal are **tremoços**. They look like small yellow beans, and are pickled in brine. Hold the **tremoço** between finger and thumb, bite into it gently to break its skin, and then squeeze to pop the content into your mouth! If you want to have a go, ask for **um prato** (a dish) **de tremoços**.

12 People are ordering drinks and snacks. The following is a list, in alphabetical order, of what they ask for. Indicate the order in which these items are mentioned on the cassette by numbering them 1, 2, 3, etc. One item on the list occurs twice on the cassette.

uma água mineral sem gás
uma bica
uma cerveja
um chá
um chá com leite
um chá de limão
um garoto
um pastel de nata
um prato de tremoços
uma sanduíche de fiambre

Check your answers in the **Key**.

13 Now *you* try ordering. Listen to your cassette and use the pause button as indicated below.

The waiter asks you what you want.

Pause   Ask for the following in Portuguese, and don't forget to say please: 'a small black coffee'; 'a small white coffee'; 'a tea with milk'; 'a lemon tea'.

Release   The waiter asks you if you want anything more.

Pause   Say 'nothing else, thank you'.

Release   The waiter repeats your order, so that you can check if it is correct.

Pause   Ask him how much it is.

Release   The waiter replies. (Don't worry at this stage if you don't quite understand how much you owe him!)

To check your part of the dialogue consult the **Key.**

14 Listen again to your cassette. People are ordering drinks, and at the end the waiter checks the order. Which items does he get wrong? (See **Key** for answer.)

Maria	Faz favor!
Empregado	Que desejam?
Maria	Um garoto, se faz favor.
Jaime	Um chá de limão.
Margarida	Uma bica.
Alberto	Um chá.
Fátima	Uma bica.
Jorge	Um chá com leite.
Empregado	Mais alguma coisa?
Maria	Mais nada, obrigada.
Empregado	Portanto, são dois garotos, uma bica, dois chás com leite, e um chá de limão.

Portanto, são...   *So that's...*
dois   *two*

18

The next item on your cassette repeats the previous dialogue, and carries on. Maria points out the waiter's mistake – **'Não!'** – and corrects him: **'São… bicas'**. Listen carefully to the word she uses before **bicas**.

15 The words for 'one' and 'two' have both masculine and feminine forms, so if you want two small black coffees you ask for **duas bicas**, but two small white coffees are **dois garotos**. From three upwards, there is no difference: **três garotos, três bicas**.

	m.	f.
1	um garoto	uma bica
2	dois garotos	duas bicas
3	três garotos	três bicas

If you want to specify more than one thing, with words that end in a vowel (except **ão**) you simply add **s**. If the word ends in a consonant (except **l** or **m**), you add **es**. However, words ending in **s**, and not stressed on the final syllable, do not change.

1	2
um inglês	dois ingleses
uma portuguesa	duas portuguesas
um chá	dois chás
um café	dois cafés

Of course, when you add **es** to a word that already ends in **s** it affects the pronunciation. See section 5 above on the different pronunciation of **s** depending on whether it occurs at the end of a word or between two vowels.

Listen to your cassette for a few examples.

Falo português

16 **Falar** is the verb 'to speak', 'to talk'. In English, the verb sometimes varies. You say, for example, 'I/you/we/they speak', but 'he/she/it speaks'. In Portuguese, this kind of variation is much more extensive and there are more changes to be made to the verb endings. For example:

falo *I speak*
fala *you speak; he/she/it speaks*
falamos *we speak*
falam *you (plural) speak; they speak*

The word for 'I' (**eu**) cropped up at the beginning of the chapter: **eu chamo-me…** ('my name is…', or, more literally, 'I am called…'). However, the words for 'I', 'you', etc., are usually omitted since to a large extent the ending of the verb shows who is doing what. And often it is clear from the situation whether, for example, **fala** means 'you speak' or 'he speaks'.

If you want to know more about verbs at this stage, consult **Grammar 9**.

Asking questions

17 Earlier in the unit you learned how to ask:

What is your name? Como é que se chama?
Where are you from? Donde é?
How much is it? Quanto é?

And how a waiter might ask you what you want:

Que deseja?
Que desejam?

Ways of asking questions with 'when', 'which', etc., will come later. Meanwhile, other kinds of questions can be asked in a simple way.

18

People are asking each other their nationality and what languages they speak. Listen carefully to the different tone of voice in the questions and answers.

Rosa	Bom dia.
Mark	Bom dia.
Rosa	Você é inglês?
Mark	Sim, sou inglês.
Rosa	Mas fala português?
Mark	Falo inglês e português.

mas *but*

19

Luís	Boa tarde.
Mary	Boa tarde.
Luís	Vocês são portuguesas?
Mary	Não, não somos portuguesas. Somos irlandesas.
Luís	Mas falam português muito bem!
Mary	Obrigada. Você fala inglês?
Luís	Não, não falo inglês. Só falo português.

são *you (plural) are*
são? *are you?*
somos *we are*
só *only*

20

Angus	Boa noite.
Carlos	Boa noite.
Angus	Você não é português?
Carlos	Não. Sou moçambicano. Sou de Maputo.
Angus	Em Moçambique falam português?
Carlos	Com certeza, falamos português. E vocês, donde são?
Angus	Somos escoceses.
Carlos	Falam inglês?
Angus	Falamos.

com certeza *certainly, of course*

> Where in English you ask a question by beginning *'Do you…?'*, in Portuguese you simply use a rising tone of voice.
>
> **Fala português**   *He/she/you speak(s) Portuguese*
> **Fala português?**   *Does he/she* } *speak Portuguese?*
>   *Do you*
>
> In order to say you don't do something, put **não** in front of the verb:
>
> **Não falo inglês**   *I don't speak English*

21

18   Listen to your cassette again and repeat the questions being asked. Each question is asked twice, with a pause in between.

Listen carefully to the tone of voice and try to imitate it.

In Portuguese, as in English, answers to this kind of question tend not to be simply a bald 'yes' or 'no'. Where in English the reply would be 'I do', 'Yes, I do', or 'No, I don't', in Portuguese you use the verb that is in the question:

Question   Fala português?
Answer   Falo
        Falo, sim
or   Não, não falo

22

19   Someone introduces herself and interviews several other people. Tick the appropriate box below to indicate where each person is from and which language(s) he/she speaks. (See **Key** for answers.)

	É de:				Fala:	
	Dublim	Londres	Lisboa	São Paulo	inglês	português
John						
Maria						
Marta						
Sónia						
Pedro						

Resumo

This section is a brief summary of the basic items in the unit. Check that you are familiar with these, and if necessary refer back to the parts of the unit that deal with them.

To greet someone, and when taking leave of someone:

a.m. until lunch-time	**Bom dia**
p.m. until dark	**Boa tarde**
from after dark	**Boa noite**

| To ask someone's name: | **Como (é que) se chama?** |
| To tell someone your name: | **Chamo-me...** |

| To ask someone where (s)he is from: | **Donde é?** |
| To say where you are from: | **Sou de...** |

To say what nationality you are: **Sou** { **português** / **portuguesa** }

To call the waiter: **Faz favor!**

Being asked what you want:	**Que deseja(m)?**
And if you want anything else:	**Mais alguma coisa?**
To say 'Nothing else':	**Mais nada**

To order something:
um copo de água
uma bica
dois chás
duas cervejas
três garotos
} **se faz favor**

To say 'Thank you', { if you are a man: **Obrigado** / if you are a woman: **Obrigada** }

To ask how much something is: **Quanto é?**

To ask the 'Do you...?' type of question, simply use the appropriate intonation: **Fala inglês?**

To say you don't do something: **Não falo inglês**

Vocabulário

escocês	um garoto	um pastel
galês	um galão	uma sanduíche
inglês		o fiambre
irlandês	um chá { com leite / sem leite / de limão }	uma torrada
moçambicano		a manteiga
	uma cerveja	
eu	uma água mineral { com gás / sem gás }	sim
você		com certeza
	fresco	não
um café	natural	
uma bica		muito
uma meia	um copo	e
de leite	um prato	mas
		ou

Mais alguma coisa?

Here are a few exercises for you to try. They are intended to help you learn rather than to test you. So don't worry if you have problems. Check your answers in the **Key**.

1 Complete the following dialogue by filling each gap with the missing word.

David	Bom............... Como é que.............. chama?
João	Chamo-...............João.
David	É português?
João	Sou. Sou.............. Lisboa. E você?
David	Eu sou.............. Sou de Edimburgo.

2 Complete the dialogue below by putting one of the following words in each gap, in the way that makes best sense.

alguma	é	natural	um
com	favor	que	uma
de	mineral		

Empregado	Boa tarde. .... desejam?
Matilde	.... cerveja, e.............. prato de tremoços, se faz favor.
Rui	Um chá.............. limão e uma torrada.............. manteiga.
Empregado	Mais.............. coisa?
Rui	E uma água.............. .
Empregado	Fresca ou.............. ?
Rui	Fresca.

Later...

Rui	Faz..............!

Waiter approaches...

Rui	Quanto..............?

3 You may like to try this puzzle.

Clues
1. You'd buy one in 11 down.
2, 3 and 4. Black tea.
5. The opposite of **natural.**
6. You speak this language already.
7. You get it from the tap – but not **com gás.**
8. Say this when the waiter brings you what you have ordered.
9 and 10. Nothing more!

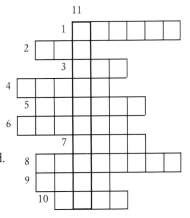

If your answers to 1-10 are correct, the vertical column numbered 11 will spell a kind of café. Leave the first clue until near the end.

The Portuguese-speaking world

To understand Portugal and the Portuguese today, you need to know something of their past. Who are the Portuguese? Part of the answer is that they are definitely not Spanish, even if they are related. There is a Portuguese saying *De Espanha nem bom vento nem bom casamento* – 'from Spain come neither fair winds nor good marriages'. This sums up an age-old suspicion of the larger neighbour who has invaded from time to time through the centuries, threatening Portugal's survival as an independent state. Cut off from the rest of Europe by an often hostile Spain, the Portuguese have turned westwards towards the Atlantic.

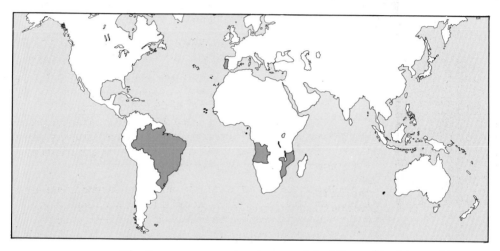

The Portuguese were the pioneers of the 'discovery' of the world beyond Europe. From the early fifteenth century, Portuguese voyagers began to explore out into the unknown waters of the Atlantic, reaching Madeira and the Azores, and down the west coast of Africa. By the end of the fifteenth century Vasco da Gama had opened up the sea-route to India, via the **Cabo da Boa Esperança** – the Cape of Good Hope, as it became in English. Throughout the sixteenth century the Portuguese set up a vast network of trading-posts in the East, from Moçambique to Japan, bringing back to Europe spices, silks, gold and precious stones.

In the late sixteenth and early seventeenth centuries the Portuguese dominance of trade in the East was lost to rival maritime powers – England and Holland – and Portugal turned its attention more towards Brazil, discovered in 1500 by Álvares Cabral. The early settlers had established sugar-plantations, which became the basis of the economy, using slaves brought from the west coast of Africa, and had exploited **pau-brasil,** the valued brazilwood which gave the country its name. But from the early eighteenth century until a few decades before its independence in 1822, Brazil's main importance to Portugal lay in its gold and precious stones.

This long maritime past and contact with the tropics are central to the Portuguese sense of national identity, of who and what they are as a

(top) Lisbon and the River Tagus

(above) Manueline window, Convento de Cristo, Tomar

nation. You will find evidence of this all around you in Portugal. For example, the ornate decoration of sixteenth century Manueline architecture features ropes and other naval motifs, such as the armillary sphere – an early navigational instrument which also appears on the Portuguese flag. The opening words of the national anthem are *Heróis do mar, nobre povo…* – 'Heroes of the sea, noble people…'. The sea-faring tradition is also represented in the characteristic patterns of the pavements in Lisbon and other cities. Even the palm-trees, which add to the dignity of public buildings and gardens, suggest a nostalgia for the historic connection with the tropics.

The Portuguese have a special word for nostalgia – **saudade**. **Saudade** is a longing for whatever is absent – far-off places, times, people, home. This feeling is expressed in some of the **fados,** the Lisbon songs developed out of an African and Brazilian musical tradition. However, it would be wrong to suggest that the Portuguese are a nation of sentimental dreamers, constantly looking back to a lost past of imperial splendour. Many Portuguese have a healthy scepticism about such sentiments.

Lisbon: the 16th-century Torre de Belém evoked the period of the Discoveries

25

2 QUE DESEJA?

In Unit 1 you learned how to use **bom dia, boa tarde** and **boa noite,** both to greet people and when taking leave of them. In Unit 2 you will learn what to say in encounters of various kinds with other people: how to say 'How are you?', how to interrupt someone in order to ask a question, how to apologise, and how to ask 'May I?'.

In Unit 1 you also learned a simple way to ask for things — naming what you want and adding **se faz favor.** This Unit will deal with further aspects of ordering what you want: how to ask what is available, and say what you would like.

How are you?

1 In these four dialogues, people are greeting each other and asking 'How are you?' (**Como está?**). Listen particularly to how this question is answered.

Filipe	Bom dia.
Jaime	Bom dia.
Filipe	Como está?
Jaime	Bem obrigado. E você?
Filipe	Estou bem, obrigado.

Sr. Alves	Boa tarde. Como está?
Sr. Reis	Boa tarde. Estou bem, obrigado. E o senhor?
Sr. Alves	Estou bem, obrigado.

E o senhor?   *And you?*

Sra. D. Maria	Boa noite.
Sr. Coelho	Boa noite.
Sra. D. Maria	Como está?
Sr. Coelho	Bem obrigado. E a senhora?
Sra. D. Maria	Estou bem, obrigada.

E a senhora?   *And you?* (addressing a woman)

Sr. Lopes	Bom dia. Como estão?
Sr. Dias	Bom dia. Estamos bem, obrigado. E os senhores, como estão?
Sr. Lopes	Muito bem, obrigado.

E os senhores, como estão?   *And how are you?* (plural)

To say   { to one person: **Como está?**
'How are you?' { to more than one person: **Como estão?**

To say *'(I'm / We're) fine, thank you'*:

(Estou / Estamos) bem, { obrigado
                            { obrigada

---

2   You may have noticed that where English uses the verb 'to be' Portuguese has two verbs. You say **sou português** (the verb **ser**), but **estou bem** (the verb **estar**). Each of these verbs is used in different circumstances and you will gradually become familiar with how each one is used. Further guidance will be given later.

3   In English we talk to people in a more or less formal way, according to how well we know them, and mostly we do this without thinking. Sometimes we are not sure if we should use the person's first name, or say 'Mr...' or 'Mrs...'.

In Portuguese, this kind of problem is more complicated: you show different degrees of formality and politeness by using the appropriate word for 'you'. Fortunately, as is explained below, you can often avoid the problem simply by omitting the word for 'you'.

The most formal way of addressing people is:

	(one person)	(more than one)
(masculine)	**o senhor**	**os senhores**
(feminine)	**a senhora**	**as senhoras**

O senhor é português?
A senhora é brasileira?   *Portuguese?*
Os senhores são angolanos?   *Are you* *Brazilian?*
As senhoras são moçambicanas?   *Angolan?*
                                         Mozambican?

You address people in this way when you don't know them well.

O senhor and **a senhora** are the words for 'the gentleman' and 'the lady'. **Senhor** (abbreviated as **Sr.**), followed by a surname, also means 'Mr' – e.g. **Sr. Rodrigues** (Mr. Rodrigues). However, for 'Mrs' and 'Miss' you say **Senhora Dona (Sra. D.)** followed by the first name, or by both the first name and the surname – e.g. **Sra. D. Maria Cabral** (Mrs / Miss Cabral). In Portugal there is no distinction between 'Mrs' and 'Miss', so really **Sra. D.** is the equivalent of 'Ms'.

Você

Você usually indicates greater familiarity with the other person. You use it with someone you can chat to in a friendly way and when you feel you are on an equal footing with the person. For example, you might use **você** in talking to a colleague at work, or to someone introduced to you by a mutual friend.

When a verb is used with **você**, it has the same ending as it would have with **o senhor**, e.g. **Você fala português? Vocês falam inglês?**

The use of **você** varies in different parts of Portugal. It is used in Lisbon, for example, but not in the north of Portugal.

27

Tu

This is another word for 'you' that you may come across. **Tu** implies intimacy. It is used, for example, in the family between brothers and sisters, and between close friends. It is also used, even on first acquaintance, between people who identify each other as belonging to a particular social group (e.g. children, or students). You are unlikely to need to use it yourself in the early stages and, since it requires slightly different verb endings, it will not be practised in the course. However, if you want to know more about it, the verb forms that correspond to **tu** are given in **Grammar 9.2** and **9.3**.

The word for 'you' is usually omitted if it is clear from the situation what is meant. For example, in theory **É português?** might mean 'Are you Portuguese?', 'Is he Portuguese?' or 'Is it Portuguese?'. However, it will normally be clear from the conversation which meaning is intended.

In Brazil, all of this is simpler: you can use **você** (or **vocês** for the plural) with anyone, regardless of how well you know them.

4 Before trying out some more greetings yourself, listen again to dialogues 23-26 on your cassette.

Now *you* have a go. Each of the next two items gives you one side of a dialogue, with pauses for you to reply. If you need longer pauses, use your pause button.

First, someone will greet you.
Reply using the same greeting.

Next, you will be asked how you are.
Reply, and ask the other person how he or she is. (Use the formal way of saying 'you', and remember to add the appropriate ending if you are talking to a woman.)

See **Key** to check your part in these dialogues.

'Have you (got) a…?'

5 Two groups of people are looking for a table (**uma mesa**) in a restaurant (**um restaurante**). Listen out for how they say 'Have you (got) a…?' and for the waiter's reply.

Celeste	Boa noite.
Empregado	Boa noite.
Celeste	Tem uma mesa para três pessoas?
Empregado	Tenho, sim. Pode ser esta?
Celeste	Está bem, obrigada.

para três pessoas *for three people*
Pode ser esta? *How about this one?* (literally *'Can it be this one?'*)

Rui	Boa tarde. Têm uma mesa para quatro pessoas?
Empregado	Só temos aquela. Pode ser?
Rui	Está bem, obrigado.

quatro *four*
Só temos aquela   *We only have that one*

To ask *'Have you (got) a...?'* or *'Have you (got) any...?'*:

Tem...?   (referring to one person)
Têm...?   (referring to more than one person)

Tem { **uma mesa?** **água mineral?**   *Have you (got)* { *a table?* *any mineral water?*

The reply is likely to include **tenho** or **temos**:

Tenho, sim   *Yes, I have*
Temos, sim   *Yes, we have*
Não, não tenho   *No, I haven't*
Não, não temos   *No, we haven't*

Now try asking what is available. You are doing some shopping, but the items you need are not on display. Say: 'Please, have you (got) any...?'

1. tea   3. ham
2. butter   4. coffee

If you need help to recall the Portuguese words, consult the **Vocabulário** in Unit 1.

To check, listen to the cassette and / or consult the **Key**.

31

How many?

6 You already know how to ask 'How much is it?' (If you need to remind yourself, consult Unit 1, section 8.)

32

In the next two dialogues listen particularly to how the waiter asks 'How many are you?' or 'For how many people?'

Carlos	Faz favor. Tem uma mesa?
Empregado	Quantos são?
Carlos	Somos cinco.
Empregado	Pode ser esta?… ou aquela?
Carlos	Esta está bem, obrigado.

33

Teresa	Como está?
Empregado	Bem, obrigado. E a senhora?
Teresa	Estou bem, obrigada. Tem uma mesa?
Empregado	Para quantas pessoas?
Teresa	Para seis.
Empregado	Só um momento… Tenho, sim. Pode ser aquela?
Teresa	Está bem, obrigada.

seis *six*
Só um momento *Just a moment*

Asking and answering *'How much?'* (**Quanto?**) and *'How many?'*
(**Quantos?**):

Quanto é?	**São vinte (20$00) escudos.**
Quantos são?	**Somos seis.**
Para quantas pessoas?	**Para cinco.**

This and that

7 In the last few dialogues the words **esta** and **aquela** have cropped up, referring to particular tables.

Specifying 'this' and 'that':

this…	that…
(m.) **este vinho**	**aquele café**
(f.) **esta cerveja**	**aquela mesa**

Or simply:

this one	that one
(m.) **este**	**aquele**
(f.) **esta**	**aquela**

34-37

8 In each of the next four items on your cassette someone asks for a table for à specific number of people. How many people are there in each group? Write the word in Portuguese and check your answer in the **Key.**

Group 1 ....　　Group 3 ....
Group 2 ....　　Group 4 ....

38

9 Now find a table for yourself. It's late afternoon, and you and a friend would like to **lanchar.** You go to your favourite café.

Your cassette gives you one side of the dialogue with the waiter. Complete the dialogue by speaking your part, indicated below by **você**. You may want to rehearse your part before you begin. Use the pause button if you need extra time to reply.

As you go in, the café seems rather full. You spot the friendly waiter that you know from previous visits...

Empregado	Boa tarde. Como está?
Você	....
Empregado	Muito bem, obrigado.
Você	*(Ask him if he has a table for two people.)*
	....
Empregado	Só um momento... Tenho aquela. Pode ser?
Você	*(Say: 'That's fine, thank you.')*
	....
Empregado	Que desejam?
Você	*(Ask for two beers and two ham sandwiches.)*
	....

39

To check your part, carry on with the cassette which will give you the full dialogue. If you want to practise writing Portuguese, write down what you have been speaking and then check it in the **Key**.

'Excuse me'... 'Sorry!'... 'May I?'

10 As you may have guessed from the number of ways of saying 'you', the Portuguese in general are extremely polite and very much aware of each other's presence. Right from the beginning you will need a few phrases to use in public places — perhaps to make your way towards a crowded bar, or to say 'sorry' if you step on someone's foot!

40

Three different people interrupt someone in order to ask a question. Listen to the word used to introduce the question.

Desculpe covers two situations. You begin with **Desculpe** (or **Faz favor**) if you need to interrupt someone to ask something.

Desculpe is also the word for 'sorry', if you accidentally cause pain or inconvenience. The answer, you hope, will be **Não faz mal** or **Não tem importância** — 'That's all right', 'It doesn't matter'.

41

Fátima is trying to make her way along a crowded Lisbon bus to get off at the next stop. Listen to how she says 'excuse me'.

Com licença, which literally means 'With (your) permission', is used when you need to ask someone to move out of your way. The answer will be **Faz favor.**

Com licença is also useful in cafés and restaurants if, for example, you need to take a free chair from a table that is already occupied. As you lay hands on the chair, you say **Com licença** and add **Posso?** — 'May I?': **Com licença. Posso?**

Finally, you may hear **Com licença** used as a way of ending a conversation — meaning something like 'Excuse me. I must go now' or 'Excuse me. I must get back to what I was doing'.

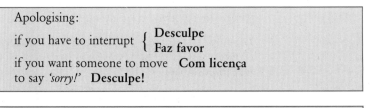

Apologising:

if you have to interrupt { **Desculpe** / **Faz favor**

if you want someone to move   **Com licença**
to say *'sorry!'*   **Desculpe!**

Asking permission:

Posso?   *May I?*
Podemos?   *May we?*

11 You have invited five friends for dinner in a rather crowded restaurant, and you need to find a table. The procedure is the same as in section 9. Again, you may like some rehearsal before you begin.

If you want to practise writing Portuguese, write the phrases in after you have gone through the whole scene speaking your part.

As you approach, a customer is blocking the doorway:

Você (*Persuade him to move.*)

....

Cliente 1 Faz favor.

As you go in you bump into another customer on her way out...

Você (*Apologise.*)

....

Cliente 2 Não faz mal.

The waiter approaches...

Empregado Boa noite.
Você (*Greet him and ask if he has a table.*)

....

Empregado São cinco?
Você (*Give the appropriate answer — and don't forget to include yourself in the group!*)

....

Empregado Pode ser esta mesa?
Você (*Accept his suggestion.*)

....

You discover there are only five chairs, and the waiter has disappeared...

Você (*Ask one of the people at the next table if you may take one of their free chairs.*)

....

Cliente 3 Faz favor.

Now carry on with your cassette. You will hear how the above dialogues might have gone.

To check your part of the dialogues, consult the **Key.**

Sounds Portuguese

12 If you need to revise nasal sounds or the various sounds that are represented by **s,** turn back to Unit 1, sections 3 and 5.

Apart from **s,** there are a number of other consonants in Portuguese that may cause some confusion if you try to pronounce them as they would be pronounced in English. Listen to the following words, and notice the sounds that are represented by the letters in bold print. Repeat each word in the pause.

ca**f**é	gre**lh**ado *(grilled)*
cinco	se**nh**or
li**c**en**ç**a	**qu**anto
dese**j**a	**qu**e

c Before **a, o,** and **u, c** sounds like the **c** in 'car'. E. g. **café, como.**
Before **e** and **i, c** sounds like the **s** in 'some'. E. g. **cinco, você.**

ç Always pronounced like the **s** in 'some'. E. g. **licença, Moçambique.**

j Like the **s** in 'measure'. E. g. **deseja, cerveja.**

lh Like the **lli** in 'million'. E. g. **grelhado, alho** *(garlic).*

nh Like the first **n** in 'union'. E. g. **senhor, tenho.**

qu Before **a, qu** sounds like the **qu** in 'quality'. E. g. **quanto, quatro.**
Before **e** and **i, qu** sounds like the **c** in 'car'. E. g. **que, aquele.** Except in the word for 'fifty' — **cinquenta** — where it sounds like the **qu** in 'quality'.

If you want some more practice, the above examples are recorded on your cassette. Listen and imitate.

A comida portuguesa

13. Portuguese food is distinctive and varied, with many regional specialities that have come out of local traditions and ingredients. For example, **Tripas à moda do Porto** (Tripe Oporto Style) — a dish which has led to the inhabitants of the northern city being known popularly as **os tripeiros** — the tripe-sellers. (Natives of Lisbon are nicknamed **alfacinhas** — little lettuces.) Or there is **Carne de porco à alentejana** (Pork Alentejo Style), a delicious dish that combines pork and clams.

For centuries, the pig has been a very important animal in the rural economy of Portugal, as in other peasant communities in Europe. The annual slaughter (**a matança do porco**), usually some time between December and Easter, is still a major event in the winter calendar of many farms and villages. In one form or another pork has an important place in Portuguese fare. In the Bairrada region, north of Coimbra, many restaurants specialise in **leitão assado** (roast sucking pig). Then there is cured ham (**presunto**) and various kinds of cured sausages (**chouriço** and **paio,** for example), which evolved in the days before refrigeration as a means of preserving pork.

Some parts of the pig are used in **feijoada,** bean stew made with dried **feijão,** and including **morcela** (black pudding) and pork knuckle. The Portuguese settlers took **feijoada** to Brazil, where it has become a national dish, using black beans (**feijão preto**) and with tropical trimmings — **farofa** or **farinha de mandioca** (manioc flour), which is sprinkled on top.

Fishing has always been a major activity, and fish (**o peixe**) and sea-food (**o marisco**) are among the most interesting aspects of Portuguese cuisine. Outside Portugal, perhaps the best known Portuguese fish is the sardine (**a sardinha**). Fresh grilled sardines (**sardinhas assadas**) are certainly popular in Portugal, especially at beach restaurants or for an open air sardine barbecue (**uma sardinhada**). But if there is a single 'national fish' it is **o bacalhau,** the dried cod that you will see hanging in old-fashioned grocers or sold in packs in supermarkets. It is said that there are 365 ways of cooking **bacalhau,** a recipe for every day of the year. On one special occasion, the traditional Christmas Eve dinner (**a consoada**), a simple **bacalhau** dish is the centre of the meal, accompanied by cabbage (**couve**) and boiled potatoes (**batatas cozidas**).

If you would like to try a recipe for **bacalhau,** you will find one later in the book (**Antologia**) — Chefe Silva's **Bacalhau na Cataplana.**

Of course, food is a large subject, and the vocabulary involved is large too. So in the following sections don't try to learn the vocabulary for different dishes all at once. Concentrate on the phrases that will help you to communicate with the waiter, such as 'I'd like a…', or 'A half portion of…, please'. Later, as you acquire new words for different dishes, you can add them to the basic phrase: 'I'd like a pork chop', 'A half portion of **feijoada**'.

Ordering

14 In the next three dialogues various people are ordering drinks or food. Listen particularly to how they ask for what they want.

Vítor is ordering a draught beer (**uma imperial**) and a dish of **tremoços.**

Empregado	Boa tarde. Que deseja?
Vítor	Queria uma imperial e um prato de tremoços, se faz favor.
Empregado	Mais alguma coisa?
Vítor	Mais nada, obrigado.

Luís and Matilde are ordering a meal. Luís asks for **febras de porco** (lean pork) and Matilde **costeletas de vitela** (veal chops). Matilde also orders **caldo verde** (literally 'green soup', a tasty soup made from a type of cabbage).

Empregado	Boa tarde. Que desejam?
Luís	Boa tarde. Queria febras de porco, se faz favor.
Empregado	Para a senhora?
Matilde	Eu queria um caldo verde e costeletas de vitela.
Empregado	E para beber?
Luís	Duas imperiais, se faz favor.

E para beber? *And to drink?*

Inês is ordering for herself and a friend. They both want **arroz de marisco** (sea-food rice).

Empregado	Faz favor. Que desejam?
Inês	Queríamos o arroz de marisco.
Empregado	Para os dois?
Inês	Sim. E uma salada mista.
Empregado	E para beber?
Inês	Têm vinho da casa?
Empregado	Temos, sim senhora. Tinto ou branco?
Inês	Branco. E bem fresco, se faz favor… Ah! Também queria uma água mineral sem gás.

vinho da casa   *house wine*
tinto   *red (only when talking of wine)*
branco   *white*
bem fresco   *nice and cool*
também   *also*

> To ask for what you want, begin **Queria**... or **Queríamos**...:
>
> **Queria**... *I'd like*...
> **Queríamos**... *We'd like*...

More than one

15 If you need to refresh your memory on how to specify more than one thing by adding **s** or **es** to the word, have a look at Unit 1, section 15.

In the previous dialogues Vítor asked for **uma imperial** (a draught beer), but Luís ordered **duas imperiais** (two draught beers). When a word ends in **l,** you usually form the plural by dropping the **l** and substituting **is.**

uma imperial	duas imperiais
água mineral	águas minerais
um pastel	dois pastéis
o hotel	os hotéis
um rissol *(a rissole)*	três rissóis

If you want more guidance at this stage on forming plurals, see **Grammar 5.2.**

16 Now order some drinks and snacks. The pattern is the same as in sections 9 and 11. Before you begin, it may help if you look again at **Resumo** and **Vocabulário** in Unit 1.

You are at a café table with a friend.

Você　(Call the waiter.)

....

Empregado　Boa tarde. Que desejam?
Você　(Order two glasses of red wine. Begin: 'We'd like...')

....

Empregado　Mais alguma coisa?
Você　(Ask him if he has any rissoles.)

....

Empregado　Tenho, sim. Quantos?
Você　(Say: 'I'd like four, please.')

....

Check your answers on the cassette and / or in the **Key.**

17 This time you are in a **pastelaria,** again ordering for yourself and a friend.

Empregado　Que desejam?
Você　(You want a black tea and a small white coffee.)

....

The waiter turns away. You have forgotten to order a **pastel de nata** *for each of you.*

37

Você	*(Call him back.)*

....

Empregado	Desejam mais alguma coisa?
Você	*(Apologise and tell him you'd also like two custard pastries.)*

....

Empregado	Mais nada?
Você	....

Check your answers on the cassette and / or in the **Key**.

Quantity control

18 Portuguese helpings are often very generous, so it's useful to know how to control the quantity being offered or served.

Álvaro asks the waiter if a half portion of fish stew is enough for one person. The waiter thinks it might be. Listen to how Álvaro then orders a half portion, and later a half bottle of wine.

Álvaro	Queria a caldeirada. Meia dose dá para uma pessoa?
Empregado	Depende. Acho que sim.
Álvaro	Então, meia dose.
Empregado	E para beber? Uma garrafa de vinho tinto?
Álvaro	Meia garrafa, se faz favor.

Acho que sim.   *I think so.*
uma garrafa   *a bottle*

The waitress in Pedro's hotel is convinced he needs to eat more. Listen to how he attempts to persuade her that he has had enough.

Empregada	Ó senhor! Então, não come mais feijoada?
Pedro	Obrigado. Não quero mais.
Empregada	Não quer mais este bocadinho?
Pedro	Chega! Não quero mais, obrigado.

não come…?   *won't you eat…?*
quero   *I want*
um bocadinho   *a little bit*

To ask for a {	half portion of…	**Meia dose de…**
	half bottle of…	**Meia garrafa de…**
To say {	'That's enough'	**Chega.**
	'I don't want any more'	**Não quero mais.**

Selecting

19 The menu (**a lista** or **a ementa**) is usually set out under a number of headings, such as:

(as) entradas *(starters)*	(a) sobremesa *(afters)*
(as) sopas	(o) doce
(os) peixes	(a) fruta
(as) carnes *(meats)*	(o) queijo *(cheese)*
(os) ovos *(eggs)*	

38

You will encounter on menus a number of very short words which at first sight may be puzzling: **ao, à, no, na, do, da.** For example, **amêijoas ao natural** (literally 'clams in the natural way' — i.e. with nothing added), **bacalhau à Gomes de Sá** (cod in the style of Gomes de Sá), **no churrasco** (on the spit), **na brasa** (over the embers — i.e. grilled), **vinho da casa** (literally, wine of the house). These very short words are in fact contractions of two words — e.g. **da = de + a** (of the).

You will come across this process of contraction frequently, so it is worth noting how it works. A common example is when the word for 'the' comes immediately after one of the following: **a** (usually meaning 'to', except on menus), **em** (in, on) and **de** (of, from). For a fuller illustration, consult **Grammar 2.2** and **2.4**.

20 Common forms of cooking are:

assado *(roast or grilled)*   frito *(fried)*
cozido *(boiled or stewed)*   grelhado *(grilled)*

In Portuguese, a descriptive word (an adjective) usually comes after the word it refers to — the opposite of English.

vinho tinto   **lulas** *(squid)* **fritas**
caldo verde   **cerveja fresca**
batatas cozidas   **arroz doce** (literally 'sweet rice' — a dessert)

For further guidance on adjectives, consult **Grammar 6.1-6.4.**

39

21 Two couples have met for lunch (**o almoço**). The first part of their menu is given below. Most of the words you haven't met before are translated.

First read through the menu.

Then listen to the cassette, more than once if necessary.

1. Tick the items that people choose.
2. At the end, what wine do they order, and how much?

Check your answers in the **Key.**

Don't worry if you don't understand all the dialogue. Listen out for the words that signal that something is being ordered: **queria**..., **para mim**... (for me...).

EMENTA   Prato do Dia: Bacalhau assado
(Dish of the day)

Sopa: Caldo verde

Peixe: Filetes de pescada *(hake)*
            Linguados *(sole)* grelhados
            Lulas fritas
            Rissóis de camarão   *(shrimp)*
            Trutas grelhadas

Carne: Bife *(steak)* à casa
            Carne de porco à Alentejana
            Espetada mista *(mixed kebab)*
            Febras de porco
            Frango piri-piri *(chicken in a hot chilli sauce)*

Omeletas: Simples *(plain)*
            Cebola *(onion)*
            Paio
            Presunto
            Queijo

Vinho da casa

22 Now they choose a dessert. Once again, listen and tick their choices. (See **Key** to check.)

Doce: Arroz doce
            Bolo de amêndoa *(almond cake)*
            Mousse de chocolate
            Pudim flan *(caramel custard)*
            Torta de ananás *(pineapple tart)*

Fruta: Laranja *(orange)*
            Maçã *(apple)*
            Melão
            Pêssego *(peach)*

Queijo: Queijo da Serra (literally *Mountain Cheese* — a popular, and now expensive cheese from the **Beira Alta**).

23 You have gone to the **Cervejaria da Trindade** for lunch. Here is a brief extract from the full menu. Study this and the instructions that follow before you begin to order.

Sopa
Caldo verde

Prato do dia
Feijoada à Trindade

Peixes
Espetada mista de peixe
Lulas grelhadas
Bacalhau à Brás
Linguado

Carnes
Bife à Trindade
Gulache à Trindade
Espetada mista
Carne de porco à Alentejana

Frutas
Maçã assada
Melão
Ananás

Doces
Tarte de laranja
Mousse de chocolate

The waiter asks you what you want.
Ask for **caldo verde** *and grilled squid.*
Listen to the waiter.

Ask for half a bottle of white wine.
Listen to the waiter.

When you finish your first two courses the waiter approaches again and asks a question.
Ask for melon and coffee.
Listen to the waiter

You finish your meal. Call the waiter and ask for the bill (**a conta***).*
Listen to the waiter.

24 You return to the **Cervejaria da Trindade** for dinner — **o jantar.**
Follow the same pattern as above.

Listen to the waiter.

Ask for steak **à Trindade.**
Listen to the waiter.

Ask for a draught beer.
Listen to the waiter.

You finish your steak. The waiter returns and asks a question.
Ask for the orange sweet.
Listen to the waiter.

Ask for a small black coffee.
Listen to the waiter.

Resumo

To ask people how they are: { **Como está?** / **Como estão?** }

To say { 'I'm / 'We're } fine, thank you': { **Estou** / **Estamos** } **bem, obrigado / a**

To address people in a formal way, use: { **o senhor, a senhora** / **os senhores, as senhoras** }
... and less formally: **você**

To ask 'Have you (got) a / any ...?' **Tem ...?**
To say 'I / We have ...' **Tenho / Temos ...**

To ask how many of something there are: **Quantos são?**

To specify this or that thing: **este / esta ... aquele / aquela ...**
or just 'this one' or 'that one': **este / esta, aquele / aquela**

To say sorry for something you've done: **Desculpe!**
To say 'Excuse me', when interrupting: **Desculpe**
... and if someone is in your way: **Com licença**

To ask 'May I?': **Posso?**

To ask for what you want: **Queria ...** / **Queríamos ...**

To ask for a half { portion: / bottle: } **Meia** { **dose** / **garrafa** } **de ...**

To say { 'That's enough': **Chega** / 'I don't want any more': **Não quero mais** }

To specify more than one (words ending in **l**), usually change **l** to **is**, e.g. **dois hotéis**

To use an adjective, place it (usually) after what it describes:
vinho verde, batatas fritas

Vocabulário

o restaurante

o jantar	o caldo	as batatas	uma garrafa
	o marisco	o arroz	
uma mesa	o peixe		o vinho
	a carne	assado	branco
uma pessoa	o frango	cozido	tinto
	um bife	frito	
quatro	uma costeleta	grelhado	a conta
cinco	a sobremesa		
seis	o doce	uma salada	só
	a fruta		também
a lista	o queijo	simples	
a ementa		misto	

Mais alguma coisa?

Complete this dialogue in a way that makes sense by putting one of the words given below in each gap. For each gap, only one of the words listed will be completely suitable. (Answers in **Key.**)

Cliente   Bom dia. (1) .... está?
Empregado   (2) .... bem, obrigado. E a senhora?
Cliente   Muito bem, obrigada. Têm uma mesa para três (3) ....?
Empregado   Só (4) .... esta. Pode ser?
Cliente   Está bem. Queria a (5) ...., faz favor.
Empregado   Com (6) .... Só um momento.

Later...

Cliente   Faz favor. Queríamos um (7) .... de marisco, uma carne de (8) .... à Alentejana, e meia (9) .... de feijoada. E (10) .... uma salada mista.
Empregado   E para (11) ....?
Cliente   Uma (12) .... de vinho branco, e uma água mineral (13) .... gás.
Empregado   Fresca ou (14) ....?
Cliente   Fresca.
Empregado   Mais alguma coisa?
Cliente   Mais (15) ...., obrigada.

arroz	estou	pessoas
beber	garrafa	porco
certeza	lista	sem
como	nada	também
dose	natural	temos

O mar

Portugal is shaped like a rough rectangle, about 600 km long
(north-south) and 200 km wide. That's over 800 km of coast, without
taking into account the islands of Madeira and the Azores. The sea (**o
mar**) has always been of vital importance to the Portuguese, and one
aspect of this was mentioned in Unit 1 — the voyages of discovery and
Portugal's long history of contact with Asia, Africa and Brazil.

The sea is also, of course, a major economic resource, and the western
and southern coasts are dotted with fishing towns where for centuries
people have engaged in both inshore and deep-sea fishing, going as far
as Newfoundland for **bacalhau.** Much of the west coast is a flat plain,
with mile upon mile of continuous beach backed by sand-dunes. So,
apart from river mouths, there are relatively few natural harbours and
the traditional form of fishing at many points on the west coast was to
launch the boat from the beach, using oxen or, more recently, tractors
to drag it back. However, there are harbours too, and the need to adapt
to different local conditions has left Portugal with a fascinating heritage
of boat design, which can be traced back to ancient Mediterranean and
Northern European origins. By the way, excellent collections of
Portuguese boats can be seen in the **Museu da Marinha** in Lisbon,
and in the Maritime Museum in Exeter.

The produce of the sea — **o peixe, o marisco** — reaches the consumer
via the auction (**a lota**), at the point where the catch is landed, and the
market (**o mercado**) — for example, **O Mercado da Ribeira** in Lisbon
where the old occupation of fish woman is now carried on by Cape
Verdeans.

If these activities, from the fishing boats themselves to the auctions
and markets, provide fascinating interest for the tourist, they are not
necessarily economically efficient. For a variety of reasons, the
Portuguese fishing industry — like agriculture in Portugal — has not kept

pace with technological change, and is suffering from the competition of more sophisticated foreign trawling fleets. And, of course, certain species of fish have seriously declined in numbers. This is the case with tunny (**o atum**), which used to be the base of an important canning industry in the Algarve, where the tunny were caught by an ingenious system of traps as they migrated along the Algarve coast to and from their spawning grounds in the Mediterranean.

In Portuguese coastal communities, especially in the centre and north, there is often a close relationship between the activities of fishing and farming. The traditional use of oxen on the beach was only one part of this. Sea-weed has long been used as a fertilizer for the land, and is still collected for this purpose in some areas — for example by the **moliceiros** in the lagoon at Aveiro (the **moliceiro** is both the boat and the boatman).

Finally, the small coastal ports are a link between the period of the Discoveries and the present. From the sixteenth century onwards, migrants set off for Brazil from such ports as Póvoa de Varzim and Viana do Castelo, establishing important economic connections across the Atlantic. Those who came back with fortunes displayed their wealth by building extravagant houses, and gave rise, in the 19th century, to a stock character in literature — **o Brasileiro.** Since the 1950s, the bulk of Portuguese emigration has been to Western Europe, and the modern migrant workers, too, build houses to show that they have been successful. This more recent emigration is a fundamental aspect of Portuguese society, and we will return to the topic in the next unit.

(left) Póvoa de Varzim (Douro Litoral): Lobster pots and stacks of sea-weed

(right) Sines fishermen in the Alentejo

45

3 PARA ONDE VAI?

This unit is mainly about travel of one kind or another. However, it begins with some language you may need not only for travel but in a variety of other situations: how to say you like something, or like doing a particular activity; how to say that something is yours — this luggage, or that taxi, for example; and how to ask 'Which is…?' 'Which is the train for Oporto?'

Oporto and the River Douro. This type of boat — the rabão — *was once used to transport port wine down river from the vineyards*

Quite a lot of the dialogues that follow are about Oporto, so a word first about the city and its name. Although it is a thriving modern city, the capital of the north and centre of the Portuguese textile industry (and, of course, of the Port wine trade), Oporto is also an ancient city, closely identified with Portugal's existence as an independent state. The name Portugal itself appears to have come from the Roman name for the town — Portus Cale. The Christian 'reconquest' of the country from the Moors began north of Oporto, in the tenth century, and the nearby town of Guimarães, associated in the twelfth century with Portugal's first king, Afonso Henriques, claims to be **o berço da nação** (the cradle of the nation).

In Portuguese, the modern name for the city is **Porto** (Harbour). However, the word for 'the' is used before any Portuguese place names that have an independent meaning, e.g. **o Porto, o Rio de Janeiro** (the River of January), **a Figueira da Foz** (the Fig-tree of the River Mouth). The **o** or **a** is sometimes omitted, for example on signs.

'I like it'

1   Francisco is interviewing people for a radio programme on tourism in Oporto and is asking visitors to the city if they like it. Listen particularly to how he asks this question.

Francisco	Bom dia.
M. N.	Bom dia.
Francisco	Como é que se chama?
M. N.	Chamo-me Margarida Neto.
Francisco	Gosta do Porto?
M. N.	Gosto muito. Gosto sobretudo da situação da cidade – do rio Douro, das pontes.

sobretudo   *above all, especially*

(If you need to remind yourself about the use of **do, da,** etc., consult **Grammar 2.4.**)

Francisco	Boa tarde.
J. M.	Boa tarde.
Francisco	Qual é o seu nome?
J. M.	O meu nome é João Magalhães.
Francisco	Donde é?
J. M.	Sou de Lisboa.
Francisco	Gosta do Porto?
J. M.	Não. Não gosto muito. É uma cidade muito escura. Prefiro Lisboa.

Qual é o seu nome   *What's your name?*

Francisco	Bom dia. As senhoras são do Porto?
Transeunte	Não. Somos de Braga.
Francisco	Gostam do Porto?
Transeunte	Gostamos. É uma cidade com muitos atractivos.
Francisco	Por exemplo?
Transeunte	Tem uma vida cultural muito interessante... Tem teatros, cinemas, boas livrarias.

um / uma transeunte   *a passer-by*
um atractivo   *an attraction, an attractive feature*
a vida   *life*

To say you (dis)like something:

(não) gosto de...
(não) gostamos de...

Gostamos de Portugal   *We like Portugal*
Você gosta da cidade?   *Do you like the city?*
Gosto do rio e das pontes   *I like the river and the bridges*
Gosto de música   *I like music*
Não gosto de chá   *I don't like tea*

---

2   Say whether or not you like the following. You will find answers for
     both alternatives in the **Key.**

'Which is my…?'

3   Francisco asked one of the people he interviewed **Qual é o seu nome?**,
     and the reply began **O meu nome é…** Let's deal first with how to say
     'my', 'mine', etc.

The words for 'my', 'mine', etc., change according to whether
what is possessed is masculine or feminine, and whether it is one
thing or more than one.

o meu
a minha } *my / mine*

Este carro é meu   *This car is mine*
A minha mesa é aquela   *My table is that one*

o nosso
a nossa } *our / ours*

Este é o nosso comboio   *This is our train*
A nossa casa é esta   *Our house is this one*

o seu
a sua } *your / yours*

O seu táxi é aquele   *Your taxi is that one*
Esta é a sua cerveja   *This is your beer*

If you are referring to more than one thing, add **s**:

Os nossos bilhetes são estes?   *Are these our tickets?*
Aquelas são as minhas malas?   *Are those my suitcases?*

If you need a fuller explanation, including how to say
'his' / 'her(s)' / 'their(s)', see **Grammar 4.**

> To ask *'Which is…?'*: **Qual é…?**
> *'Which are…?'*: **Quais são…?**
> **Qual é o meu comboio?**
> **Quais são os autocarros** *(buses)* **para Vila Nova de Gaia?**
> **Qual é a linha?** (*Which platform is it?* — literally *'Which is the line?'*)
>
> **Qual é…?** is also used to ask *'What is…?'*, UNLESS you are asking for a definition of something (E. g. *'What is a chouriço?'* **O que é um chouriço?**):
>
> **Qual é o seu nome?** *What's your name?*
> **Qual é a sua morada?** *What's your address?*
> **Qual é o seu número de telefone?** *What's your phone number?*
>
> So it's like asking, for example, 'Which (of the many possibilities) is your name, address, etc.?'.

4 Tell someone that the following are yours, beginning with the Portuguese for 'This is my…'

To check your answers listen to the cassette and / or consult the **Key**.

'I like… -ing'

5 Francisco continues his interviews. Now he is asking people who live in Oporto whether they like living there. Listen to how he puts the question 'Do you like living in Oporto?'

Francisco	Desculpe. Posso fazer-lhe umas perguntas?
Transeunte	Faz favor.
Francisco	O senhor mora aqui no Porto?
Transeunte	Moro aqui, sim.
Francisco	Gosta de morar no Porto?
Transeunte	Gosto.
Francisco	Quais são as vantagens?
Transeunte	Bom… É uma cidade muito agradável. Eu gosto muito de passear, de ir aos cafés, por exemplo.
Francisco	Muito obrigado.
Transeunte	De nada.

49

fazer uma pergunta   *to ask a question*
O senhor mora aqui?   *Do you live here?*
passear   *to stroll*
ir   *to go*

Francisco	Faz favor. Posso fazer-lhe umas perguntas?
Transeunte	Com certeza.
Francisco	O senhor é do Porto?
Transeunte	Bom. Moro aqui, mas sou de Vila Real.
Francisco	Gosta de viver aqui?
Transeunte	Não gosto muito.
Francisco	Porquê?
Transeunte	Porque não gosto de viver numa grande cidade. Tem muito trânsito, muita poluição, sobretudo às horas de ponta.
Francisco	Portanto, tem saudades da sua terra?
Transeunte	Tenho, sim.

morar   *to live (in the sense of to reside)*
viver   *to live (in other senses)*
o trânsito   *the traffic*
Porquê?   *Why?*
a hora de ponta   *rush hour*
Tem saudades da sua terra?   *Do you miss home?*

To say you like doing something, use:

Gosto de...
Gostamos de...

and add the word for the action:

Gosto de viver aqui   *I like living here*
As senhoras gostam de viajar?   *Do you like travelling?*
Gostamos de passear   *We like going for a walk*

---

6   Now try some practice. To fill each gap below, select the appropriate word from the following: **de, do, da, no, na, ao, à.**

See **Key** for answers.

1. Moro .... Porto.
2. Não gosta .... viver .... cidade?
3. Qual é o prato .... dia?
4. Gostamos .... almoçar aqui.
5. Queria as tripas .... moda .... Porto.
6. Querem o vinho .... casa?
7. Moramos .... centro .... cidade.

'I'm going by...'

7   Teresa is doing a survey of transport in the Oporto area. She is interested in finding out how people travel to work. Listen particularly to how they answer this question: **Como vai para o emprego?**

Teresa	Onde mora?	
Alberto	Moro na Avenida da Boavista.	
Teresa	Onde trabalha?	
Alberto	Trabalho numa loja na Rua de Santa Catarina.	
Teresa	Como vai para o emprego?	
Alberto	Vou de autocarro.	

Onde trabalha?   *Where do you work?*
uma loja   *a shop*
o emprego   *employment, work*

Teresa	Onde moram?	
Rui	Moramos aqui no Porto.	
Teresa	Onde trabalham?	
Rui	Trabalhamos em Aveiro.	
Teresa	Como vão para o emprego?	
Rui	Vamos de comboio.	

Teresa	Onde é que mora?	
Laura	Moro em Miragaia.	
Teresa	Onde trabalha?	
Laura	Trabalho em Matosinhos.	
Teresa	Como vai para o emprego?	
Laura	Vou no meu carro.	

Teresa	Onde moram?	
Filipe	Moramos na Ribeira.	
Teresa	Onde é que trabalham?	
Filipe	Trabalhamos em Vila Nova de Gaia.	
Teresa	Como vão para o emprego?	
Filipe	Geralmente apanhamos o autocarro, mas às vezes vamos de táxi.	

geralmente   *generally, usually*
apanhamos   *we catch*
às vezes   *sometimes*

To say what means of transport you use:

Vou
Vamos } de {
avião   *(by air)*
barco   *(by boat)*
camioneta   *(by coach)*
metro   *(on the underground)*
táxi   *(by taxi)*

BUT:

Vou a pé   *I go / am going on foot.*

To say which particular train, etc. you take / are taking:

Vou
Vamos } no {
comboio das 8.30
avião TAP, voo n.º 483   *(flight no. 483)*
meu carro

8 How are the people travelling in these pictures? Complete the caption
Vai… or **Vão…** in each case by adding two more words.

69

Check your answers on the cassette and / or in the **Key.**

Where to?

70

9 In the next three dialogues, people are taking taxis to various stations.
Listen to how they say where they want to go.

Maria is going to the station, but the taxi-driver needs to know which
one.

Maria	Boa tarde.
Taxista	Boa tarde.
Maria	Para a estação, se faz favor.
Taxista	A estação do caminho de ferro ou dos autocarros?
Maria	Do caminho de ferro.

o caminho de ferro   *the railway*

71

Ana is catching a flight to London.

Ana	Bom dia.
Taxista	Bom dia, minha senhora.
Ana	Para o aeroporto, se faz favor.
Taxista	Sim senhora. Partidas domésticas?
Ana	Não, partidas internacionais.

Partidas domésticas   *Internal departures*

72

João	Boa noite.
Taxista	Boa noite. Para onde vai?
João	Para a estação de S. Bento, se faz favor.
Taxista	Desculpe. Para onde?
João	Para a estação de S. Bento.

Para onde?   *Where to?*

> To indicate where you want to go:
>
> **Para...**
>
> **Para o Rossio**
> **Para o cinema Alvalade** } **se faz favor**
> **Para o Centro de Arte Moderna**

10 More notes on **para, onde** and a

para

You can use **para...** to a taxi driver: **Para o aeroporto, se faz favor;** or when buying a rail or bus ticket: **Para Cascais, se faz favor;** or, as a question, to ask your way to somewhere: **Para o Rossio, se faz favor?**

onde and **para onde**

Onde means 'where', referring to something stationary, e. g. **Onde trabalha?** *(Where do you work?).*

Para onde means 'where' or 'to where', when movement is involved, e. g. **Para onde vai?** *(Where are you going?).*

ir para and **ir a**

In addition to phrases like **vou para o Porto,** you will also come across **vou ao Porto.**

When you say **vou a...,** you imply you will not be staying long, e. g.: **Vou um momento ao café.**

Vou para..., on the other hand, implies that the place you mention is the end of that particular journey, or that you will be staying some time, e. g.: **Quando acabo o trabalho, vou logo para casa** *(When I finish work, I go straight home);* **Vou ao Porto e depois para Lisboa** *(I'm going to Oporto and then to Lisbon).*

73

11 Now try four trips by taxi. For each trip the pattern is as follows:

The driver asks you where you are going.
Say 'To the...', please'.
The driver will reply.
(In the driver's replies, it is sometimes assumed that you are a man and sometimes that you are a woman.)

Your destinations are:

1 the railway station
2 the city centre
3 the bus station
4 the airport.

12 If you are buying a ticket and you say simply **Para..., se faz favor,** it will usually be assumed you want a single ticket. You might want to come back again, so in the next two dialogues listen particularly for the words for 'single' and 'return'.

Passageira	Bom dia. Queria um bilhete simples para Aveiro.
Funcionário	São trezentos escudos.
Passageira	Obrigada.
Funcionário	De nada.

Passageira	Boa tarde. Queria um bilhete de ida e volta para Cascais. Quanto é?
Funcionário	São noventa e cinco escudos.
Passageira	Obrigada.

> To ask for a single ticket to…:
>
> **Queria um bilhete simples para…**
> Or simply: **Para…, se faz favor**
>
> To ask for a return to…:
>
> **Queria um bilhete de ida e volta para…**

13 You want to buy a ticket to Coimbra. Use your pause button if you need more time to speak your part of the dialogue.

Você	*(Tell the ticket clerk your destination.)*

....

Funcionário	Simples ou de ida e volta?
Você	*(Say you want a return; ask how much it is.)*

....

Funcionário	São quinhentos e vinte escudos.
Você	*(Thank him.)*

....

Check your answer on the cassette.

Here is a slightly more complex journey, which involves dealing with two people. This time try writing your part of the dialogue. The situation is as follows (if you have difficulties with this, consult the **Key**):

14 Você está em Lisboa, num hotel na Avenida da República. Quer visitar Sintra. Os comboios para Sintra partem da estação do Rossio. Você chama um táxi.

partir *to leave*

15

Taxista	Bom dia. Para onde vai?
Você	....
Taxista	Sim senhor / senhora.
	Later...
Você	....
Taxista	São duzentos escudos.
	Shortly afterwards...
Você	....
Funcionário	Simples ou de ida e volta?
Você	....
	(Ask how much it is.)
	....
Funcionário	São noventa e cinco escudos.

Check your answer in the **Key**.

Buying tickets, of course, involves understanding prices and being able to ask for information about times. For both prices and times you need to know Portuguese numbers.

The remainder of this unit deals with time — the time of day, the names of the days of the week, and of the months. All of this, especially the numbers involved, presents you with a lot of new words. Don't try to learn them all at once. There will be opportunities for further practice later in the course, and you can refer back to this unit from time to time for revision.

'What time is it?'

16 The next item on your cassette consists of six short sections, numbered **um, dois, três,** etc. These numbers are recorded on the cassette, to help you match each section with the text.

In each section, someone asks the time and is given an answer. In some cases the answer is given in more than one way — just as in English you might say, for example, either 'seven forty-five' or 'a quarter to eight'.

Listen to the cassette, using the text and the times given to understand each section. Notice particularly the phrases you need in order to say 'It's... o'clock', 'It's a quarter past / to...', 'It's half past...', etc. You may need to use your pause button between each sequence.

um	Faz favor. Que horas são?	[7.00]
	São sete horas.	
dois	Desculpe. Tem horas?	[8.15]
	São oito e um quarto.	
	São oito e quinze.	
três	Podia-me dizer as horas, por favor?	[9.20]
	São nove e vinte.	
quatro	Faz favor. Tem horas?	[10.30]
	São dez e meia.	
	São dez e trinta.	
cinco	Podia-me dizer as horas, se faz favor?	[11.45]
	É meio-dia menos um quarto.	
	É meio-dia menos quinze.	
	São onze e quarenta e cinco.	
seis	Desculpe. Que horas são?	[1.55]
	São duas menos cinco.	
	É uma e cinquenta e cinco.	

Que horas são?   *What time is it?*
Tem horas?   *Have you (got) the time?*
Podia-me dizer as horas?   *Could you tell me the time?*

To ask someone the time: **Que horas são?**
Tem horas?
To tell someone the time: **São**...
É...

on the hour, add **horas** after the number:

São { três / oito } horas

up to half past, use **e:**

São { onze / duas / cinco } e { dez / um quarto / meia }

after half past, use **menos** (less):

São { quatro / seis } menos { vinte e cinco / um quarto }

with midday, midnight and 1.00 (which are thought of as singular) use **é** instead of **são:**

É { meio-dia / meia-noite e vinte / uma menos cinco }

---

17   Being able to cope with the time of day is partly a question of using structures such as **São**... **e**... or **São**... **menos**... It is also a question of being familiar with the numbers you need to slot into the gaps — and numbers, of course, are useful for other purposes.

Below is a list of numbers, with any that are entirely new to you given in Portuguese. Listen again to the previous item on your cassette and as you hear the numbers write them in the appropriate gap.

First try this just listening to the cassette, without looking at the numbers in the text (16 above).

You will probably still have some gaps — so try again using the text too this time.

Finally, check your answers against the numbers in **Grammar 12.** You may need your list for the next exercise, so it's important to be accurate.

1...............	11...............	21............... e um/uma
2...............	12. doze	22............... e dois/duas
3...............	13. treze	23............... e três
4...............	14. catorze	Etc. until:
5...............	15...............	30...............
6...............	16. dezasseis	31............... e um/uma
7...............	17. dezassete	32............... e dois/duas
8...............	18. dezoito	33............... e três (etc.)
9...............	19. dezanove	40...............
10...............	20...............	50...............

18 Now try saying what time it is on the following clocks. **Que horas são?**

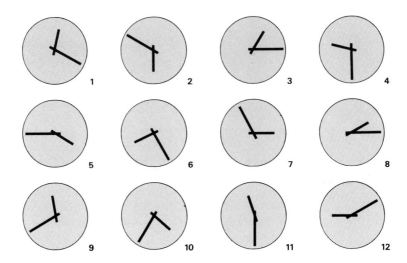

Check your answers in the **Key.**

'At what time…?'

19 António is comparing train and coach times in a travel agency (**uma agência de viagens**) before deciding how to travel. (The 24-hour clock is frequently used when giving travel times.)

Listen particularly to how António asks the times of departure and arrival.

57

António	A que horas parte o comboio?
Empregada	O comboio parte às 16.00 horas.
António	Portanto, às 4.00 da tarde… E a que horas chega?
Empregada	Chega às 19.15.
António	Às sete e um quarto… E a camioneta?
Empregada	A camioneta parte às 7.30 e chega às 9.45.
António	Da manhã?
Empregada	Da manhã, sim.
António	Então vou de camioneta. Queria um bilhete de ida e volta, se faz favor.

da tarde   *in the afternoon*
da manhã   *in the morning*

To ask *'At what time?'*:

A que horas…?
A que horas parte o comboio?   *What time does the train leave?*
A que horas chega o avião?   *What time does the plane arrive?*

To say at what time:

às…
O avião chega às dezoito e trinta

---

20 Roberta is at the railway station. See how much of the dialogue you can follow without a text. First read the questions below, then listen and answer in English. Don't worry if you don't understand all the dialogue — listen particularly for the information you need.

1. Where is she going? ....
2. Does she want a single or return ticket? ....
3. What is the fare? ....
4. What time does the train leave? ....
5. What time does it arrive? ....
6. Which platform does it leave from? ....

Check your answers in the **Key.**

Sections 21 and 22 are intended mainly for reference purposes. Don't worry if the names of the days, months and seasons are too much to remember — consult these sections whenever you want the word for a specific day or month, and you will gradually become familiar with the words.

Days of the week

21 Whereas in English the days of the week have names — Monday, Tuesday, etc. — in Portuguese, with the exception of Saturday and Sunday, the days of the week have numbers: 'second', 'third', etc.

We usually think of the week as beginning on Monday. However, it may help you to recall the Portuguese days if you think of the first day as Sunday. Then 'Monday' is **segunda-feira**, 'Tuesday' **terça-feira** etc.

o domingo	*Sunday*	a quinta-feira	*Thursday*
a segunda-feira	*Monday*	a sexta-feira	*Friday*
a terça-feira	*Tuesday*	o sábado	*Saturday*
a quarta-feira	*Wednesday*		

O and a are usually omitted, except in saying 'on Sunday(s)' etc., and often the -feira is dropped. The words are sometimes shortened by writing the '2nd' etc., as a number, e.g. 2ª-feira.

The Portuguese words for 'first', 'second' etc., are:

1st	primeiro	*4th*	quarto
2nd	segundo	*5th*	quinto
3rd	terceiro	*6th*	sexto

Note that the word for third is slightly different from the form used in terça-feira.

To ask '*(On) Which day...?*':

Em que dia...?

Em que dia vão para Londres?

To say '*on Sunday*' etc. (i.e. on a specific day):	To say '*on Sundays*' etc. (i.e. in general):
no/na...	**aos/às...**
Vamos para Londres no domingo *(We're going to London on Sunday)*	**Não trabalho aos sábados** *(I don't work on Saturdays)*
Na segunda-feira vou ao cinema *(On Monday I'm going to the cinema)*	**Às quintas almoço em casa** *(On Thursdays I have lunch at home)*

Months, seasons, dates

22   The months (**os meses**):

The seasons of the year (**as estações do ano**):

Janeiro	Julho	a Primavera
Fevereiro	Agosto	o Verão
Março	Setembro	o Outono
Abril	Outubro	o Inverno
Maio	Novembro	
Junho	Dezembro	

---

em Janeiro *in January*
na Primavera *in Spring*
no dia } **25 de Abril** } **de 1974** *on the 25th of April 1974*
a

23 Now try using the names of the days of the week. Here is an extract from the **Cervejaria da Trindade** menu which you saw in Unit 2 — the **Pratos do Dia** for an entire week.

2.ª-feira: Dobrada à Trindade   360$00
3.ª-feira: Bacalhau à Gomes de Sá   440$00
4.ª-feira: Jardineira à Trindade   360$00
5.ª-feira: Feijoada à Trindade   360$00
6.ª-feira: Arroz de polvo   370$00
Sábado: Salada à chefe   400$00

81

Listen to your cassette. You will be asked 'which day do they have...?', for each of the dishes on the above list. Answer with the Portuguese for 'on Monday' or whichever is the right day. If you wish, write your answers as well as speaking them.

1............... 4...............
2............... 5...............
3............... 6...............

Check your answers in the **Key**.

24 If you would like to practise some of the higher numbers — the hundreds — have a look at **Grammar 12.1-12.4** and then try writing out in words the price of the **Prato do Dia** for each day. Then check your answers in the **Key**.

Resumo

To say you like something: **Gosto do / da / dos / das...**

To say you like doing something: **Gosto de** { **falar português** / **viajar** / **passear** }

To say 'This is my...': { **Este é o meu...** / **Esta é a minha...** }

To ask { 'Which is...?':   **Qual é...?** / 'Which are...?':   **Quais são...?** }

To say { you go / you're going } by bus etc.:   **Vou de autocarro**

{ you're going on a / particular bus etc.: }   **Vou no autocarro no. 36**

Being asked your destination: **Para onde vai?**
To indicate your destination: **Para..., se faz favor**

To ask for a single (return) ticket to...:   **um bilhete simples (de ida e volta) para...**

To say what time it is: { **É meio-dia** / **São... horas** / **São... e...** / **São... menos...** }

	the time:	**Que horas são?**
To ask	(on) which day...?:	**Em que dia...?**
	(at) what time...?:	**A que horas...?**

	na segunda-feira
To say on which day:	**no sábado**
	no dia um de Março
	a 5 de Outubro de 1910

To say (at) what time: **às...**

Vocabulário

ir	a estação	morar
viajar	o caminho de ferro	a morada
apanhar	a linha	o telefone
um bilhete	o aeroporto	viver
uma mala		
	chegar	a vida
um autocarro	a chegada	uma vantagem
um avião		um atractivo
um barco	partir	agradável
uma camioneta	a partida	interessante
um carro	o trânsito	trabalhar
um comboio	a hora de ponta	o trabalho
um eléctrico		o emprego
um táxi	a cidade	uma loja
	o rio	
passear	a ponte	sobretudo
a pé		às vezes
		por exemplo

Mais alguma coisa?

Here is a short passage to read. Some of the expressions are explained below. You will probably find you can understand a lot of it, but if you have problems with some of the words, consult the **Glossary**.
Margarida is describing a typical working day.

Chamo-me Margarida Silva. Moro em Aveiro. Sou professora de inglês e alemão, e trabalho na Escola Secundária de José Estêvão. Normalmente levanto-me às 7.30. Tomo o pequeno almoço pelas 8.00 e saio de casa às 8.15. Costumo ir a pé para a escola, mas quando me atraso vou de autocarro. Tenho aulas das 8.30 ao meio-dia e vinte, ou 1.30. Por volta das 10.30 tomo um café com os colegas no bar da escola. Volto para casa para almoçar entre a 1.00 e a 1.30. Quando tenho aulas de tarde, almoço na escola. Trabalho em casa durante a tarde, mas quase sempre saio para fazer compras ou para ir à aula de ginástica. Janto por volta das 8.30. Às vezes vou ao cinema, mas quase sempre tenho que fazer e por isso costumo ficar em casa.

pelas... } *at about...*		
por volta das...	**uma aula** *a class*	
costumo... *I usually...*	**de tarde** *in the afternoon*	
quando me atraso *when I'm late*	**ter que fazer** *to have things to do*	61

A terra

Much of the material relating to travel in this unit has been set in Oporto. If you turn inland from the city, northwards into the Minho, or to the most north-easterly province, Trás-os-Montes (Behind the Mountains), you will be struck by the impact on people's lives of one particular form of travel — emigration.

The Portuguese voyagers of the fifteenth century opened up the sea-routes to Africa, India and Brazil, beginning an exodus — particularly to Brazil — which has continued through the centuries. In recent decades the direction of this emigration has shifted, with a flood of migrant labour to Europe in the boom years of the 1960s. Between 1960 and 1974, 1.5 million left Portugal, about a third of the labour force. In terms of population, Paris became the second largest Portuguese city.

Though emigration is by no means exclusively a northern phenomenon, it is particularly marked in the rural areas of the north, where the system of inheriting land has produced small-holdings

A Minho valley

(**minifúndios**) incapable of sustaining families without recourse to migration to the city, or emigration to more industrialised countries. Apart from problems of rural poverty, in the 1960s many thousands of Portuguese left the country clandestinely to avoid long military service in the colonial wars in Africa, or to escape from the political repression of the Salazar regime.

The phenomenon of emigration relates to a question raised in Unit 1 — who are the Portuguese? That is, emigration poses acute problems for how the Portuguese perceive their own national identity and the survival of the language and culture.

On the one hand, through the remittances (**as remessas**) that they send home, the migrant workers have a vital role in the attempt to bridge Portugal's chronic trade gap. So it is not just for reasons of patriotic

*Luís de Camões
(1524?-1580)*

sentimentality that Portugal's national day, **o Dia de Camões**
(10 June), has become, in a more democratic Portugal, **o Dia
de Camões e das Comunidades** — in honour of the communities
of migrant workers living overseas. Symbolically as well as in economic
reality, Portugal includes the millions living abroad — many of whom
return, of course, to establish themselves on their savings, or to retire,
or at the very least for the annual August holiday spent in their **terra**
— a term that, as well as meaning 'land', means 'home' (in the sense
of birth-place).

On the other hand, emigration on this scale is seen by some as a threat
to Portuguese culture. The children of the migrant worker, educated in
French or German schools, may grow up identifying more with the
host country than with Portugal. In the case of both adults and
children, permanent residence abroad 'corrupts' their language — they
come back in the summer not for their **férias** (holidays) but their
vacanças (from the French *vacances*). And the threat to language is not
simply a matter of the incorporation of a few foreign terms. For the
children, at least, there is often a real loss of competence in Portuguese.

A more visible aspect of foreign 'corruption' of Portuguese culture
is the *estilo maison* houses which the migrants build for themselves
in their villages, an ostentatious rejection of the traditional rural
architecture which, however picturesque, is perhaps associated with
the poverty that made emigration necessary in the first place.

These cultural consequences of emigration are a modern manifestation
of a much older attitude — the receptiveness of the Portuguese to the
outside world. This openness has often enriched Portuguese language
and culture, but sometimes it has its negative side too: an excessively
self-deprecating admiration for anything foreign, for anything that
comes from **lá fora** ('out there' i.e. abroad). Until recently, when
television and the cinema have brought new influences, the cultural
mecca for the Portuguese was France. As Eça de Queirós, Portugal's
greatest novelist of the nineteenth century, put it (with deliberate
exaggeration) Portugal *'é um país traduzido do francês em calão'* — a
country translated from French into slang. However, the Portuguese
ability to adapt and change in response to outside influence may prove
crucial for the country's future within the EEC.

4 ONDE É?

Unit 4 deals mainly with asking where things are located, asking the way and understanding directions. Towards the end of the unit these skills, and some others you have learned already, are applied to booking a room in a hotel. So this final part of the unit also introduces new vocabulary needed for this situation.

Before you ask 'Where is the…?', you will sometimes need to ask a prior question to discover if what you want is in fact available.

Is there a…?

1 You learned in Unit 2 how to use **Tem**…? to ask 'Have you (got) a…?' or 'Have you (got) any…?'. In the following dialogues listen particularly to how people ask 'Is there a…?' or 'Are there any…?'.

João has just arrived in a small country town (**uma vila**), and wants a hotel. He stops a woman in the street.

82

João	Desculpe. Há um hotel na vila?
Transeunte	Não, não há. Mas há uma pensão aqui na praça.
João	Obrigado.
Transeunte	De nada.

uma pensão   *a guest house*
aqui   *here*
a praça   *the square*

83

Ana Maria asks the waiter if there is a guest house nearby.

Ana Maria	Faz favor. Há uma pensão aqui perto?
Empregado	Sim senhora. Há várias pensões. A mais próxima é ali na avenida.
Ana Maria	Muito obrigada.

Évora:
the Roman temple

aqui perto   *near here*
o mais próximo   *the nearest*
ali   *there*

84

Bárbara wants to take a coach to Évora.

Bárbara	Faz favor. Há camionetas para Évora?
Funcionário	Há, sim senhora. A próxima parte às onze e um quarto.
Bárbara	Então queria um bilhete de ida e volta.
Funcionário	São quatrocentos e vinte e cinco escudos.
Bárbara	Obrigada.

o próximo   *the next one*

To ask { 'Is there a…?'   **Há um(a)…?**
{ 'Are there any…?'   **Há…?**

Há um banco aqui perto? *Is there a bank near here?*
Há pensões aqui perto? *Are there any guest houses near here?*

Notice that when enquiring about more than one thing, where English uses 'Are there any…?' Portuguese simply uses **Há…?**

---

2 Try asking what is available. If you need to revise some of the words required below, have a look at the vocabulary section at the end of Unit 3.

You are in a tourist office in Lisbon. Ask if there is / are:

1. a restaurant near here
2. trains to Sintra
3. a plane to London at 1.30
4. buses from the airport to the city centre
5. a coach at 6.30 to Setúbal
6. a guest house near here
7. trams to Belém
8. a café in the square

85

Check your answers on the cassette and / or in the **Key**.

Where is it?

3 You have already come across the fact that the English 'to be' is sometimes **ser** in Portuguese and sometimes **estar**. They are not interchangeable, and you will need one or other when talking about where things are.

86

António and Margarida have just decided to go to the Museum of Ancient Art in Lisbon. Listen particularly to how they say which street (**uma rua**) they are in at the moment, and where their car is.

Margarida	Então vamos ao Museu de Arte Antiga?
António	Está bem. Apanhamos o eléctrico?
Margarida	Onde é que estamos?
António	Estamos na Rua do Alecrim.
Margarida	O carro está muito perto. Vamos de carro.

> To ask / say where something is
>
> if you are referring to a person, or to something that can be moved, use **estar**:
>
> **Onde estamos?**
> **O carro está na praça**
> **Estão no Hotel Boa Vista**
> **O meu passaporte está na mesa**

4 Now for some practice. Complete the following phrases by filling the gap with the appropriate word for 'am', 'is' or 'are'. See **Key** to check your answers.

1. Os senhores............... no hotel?
2. O nosso carro............... na praça.
3. Eu............... em Lisboa.
4. As nossas malas............... na pensão.
5. *(We)*............... no centro da cidade.
6. A minha cerveja............... na mesa.

5 However, when you are asking about the location of things that cannot be moved, there are two different ways of saying 'Where is…?'. Listen out for them in the following dialogues.

Miguel is looking for a chemist's and stops a passer-by:

Miguel	Faz favor. Há uma farmácia aqui na vila?
Transeunte	Há uma na Rua de Santo António.
Miguel	E onde é a Rua de Santo António?
Transeunte	É esta rua aqui, em frente da igreja.
Miguel	Obrigado.

em frente de   *opposite, facing*
uma igreja   *a church*

Sofia asks her friend where there is a bank:

Sofia	Há um banco aqui perto?
José	Há vários. O mais próximo é no Largo de Camões.
Sofia	E onde fica o Largo de Camões?
José	É aquela praça ali, no fim desta rua.

um largo   *a square*
no fim (de)   *at the end (of)*

Rui stops a woman in the street to ask where the post office is:

Rui	Desculpe. Podia-me dizer onde é o correio?
Transeunte	Sim senhor. Com certeza. É em frente da estação.
Rui	Fica longe?
Transeunte	Não, fica perto. Pode perfeitamente ir a pé.
Rui	Muito obrigado, minha senhora.

Podia-me dizer…?   *Could you tell me…?*
longe *far*
perfeitamente   *perfectly well*

> **To ask / say where something is**
>
> if you are referring to a place, a building, or anything that has a permanent position, use **ser** or **ficar:**
>
> **Onde é o Banco Português do Atlântico?**
> **Onde fica uma farmácia?**
> **O correio é na Praça dos Restauradores**
> **Évora fica no Alentejo**
>
> To ask if it's far / near: É
>   Fica } longe / perto?

Ficar

Note that **ser** and **ficar** are only interchangeable when talking about where something is located. **Ficar** can have several other meanings, depending on the context: usually the meaning is related to 'to stay' or 'to be situated'.

Há, estar, ser or ficar

6 To practise using what you have learned so far in this unit, work out what's missing in the following questions (**perguntas**) and answers (**respostas**).

Write an appropriate short question for each **pergunta,** and fill in the missing word in each **resposta.**

Notice that in number 3 the question will need the word for 'my'.

1. Pergunta ………………………………………………………………………?
    Resposta O Hotel Capitol?…………… na Rua Eça de Queirós.
2. Pergunta ………………………………………………………… aqui perto?
    Resposta Uma farmácia?…………… uma no Centro Comercial *(in the Shopping Centre).*
3. Pergunta ………………………………………………………………………?
    Resposta Os seus *(your)* bilhetes?…………… na mesa.
4. Pergunta ………………………………………………………………………?
    Resposta O banco mais próximo?…………… na Avenida da Liberdade.
5. Pergunta ………………………………………………………………………?
    Resposta O nosso carro?…………… ali na praça.

Now listen to your cassette for a full version of each of the above.
(If you hear **fica** where you have suggested **é**, or vice versa, that's fine: as explained earlier, they are interchangeable when talking about where something is located.)

The answers are also given in the **Key.**

Where did you say?

7 When you ask where something is, the reply will include words to do with location, so you need to be able to understand the commonest ones. Some of these have cropped up already:

aqui   ali
perto   longe
em frente de   no fim de

Other such phrases in English are:

beside
on the left-hand side (of)   on the right-hand side (of)
in the middle (of)   between
behind   at the far end (of)

91

Listen to your cassette and use the plan of a town square to work out which English phrase above corresponds to each Portuguese phrase below. Yow will need the words **jardim** (garden) and **fonte** (fountain).

Portuguese	English
1. atrás (de)	....
2. do lado esquerdo (de)	....
3. no meio (de)	....
4. ao fundo (de)	....
5. do lado direito (de)	....
6. entre	....
7. ao lado (de)	....

Você está aqui

Now check your answers in the **Key.**

8 Carry on with your cassette. You will hear twelve statements about the plan of the square, and where things are in relation to each other. Some of the statements are true, others are false. Indicate which are true and which are false by writing **sim** or **não** below.

1...............	5...............	9...............
2...............	6...............	10...............
3...............	7...............	11...............
4...............	8...............	12...............

Check your answers in the **Key.**

Os nomes das ruas

9 So far in this unit a number of words for streets and squares have cropped up: **uma rua, uma avenida, uma praça, um largo.** Another common word is **uma estrada** — a road. In finding your way around Portuguese towns and cities you will come across several other words for different kinds of streets: **uma travessa,** usually a lane between two main roads (**atravessar** is 'to cross'); **uma calçada,** a paved (often cobbled) street; **um beco,** 'an alley' ('a dead end', in the metaphorical sense, is **um beco sem saída** — literally 'an alley without exit'). You may have noticed in previous dialogues that, unlike English, the word for 'the' is used with the names of streets, squares and other features of the urban landscape: **o Parque Eduardo VII fica ao fundo da Avenida da Liberdade** (Edward VII Park...). However, on street signs or maps the word for 'the' is omitted.

*Praça Luís de Camões
and the Camões statue*

Street names often indicate which people and events of the past are seen as important. In Lisbon, for example, there is **a Praça de Camões,** or **a Praça dos Restauradores** — the 'restorers' of Portugal's independence in 1640, after a 60-year interval of Spanish rule. The same restoration — **a Restauração** — is commemorated in the names of **a Avenida da Liberdade,** nearby, and **a Rua Primeiro de Dezembro** — a date, by the way, which is also celebrated as a national holiday (**um feriado**).

Dates occur frequently in Portuguese street names. In Lisbon there is **a Avenida 5 de Outubro,** for example, which commemorates the end of the monarchy and the proclamation of the republic in 1910. The most recent of such dates is **o 25 de Abril,** the 25th of April, 1974, when the 48-year dictatorship of Salazar and his brief successor Caetano was overthrown by a military coup. This turning-point in the recent history of Portugal is celebrated in the name of the splendid bridge over the Tagus, **a Ponte 25 de Abril** (formerly **a Ponte Salazar**), and in other names — for example, **a Avenida das Forças Armadas** (formerly **a Av. 28 de Maio,** a date associated with Salazar's rise to power).

Finding your way

10 When following instructions to go somewhere, there are a number of key words you will need to be able to recognise. Among these are the words for 'first', 'second', etc. If you want to revise these, turn to Unit 3, section 22.

93

11 On page 72 is a map of part of **a Baixa Pombalina,** the area of the city centre in Lisbon rebuilt by the **Marquês de Pombal** after the devastation of the 1755 earthquake.

Sr. Gomes works in a shop (marked * on the map) at the bottom end of **a Rua do Ouro** (Gold Street). At lunch time he takes a stroll up to **Rossio** square for a coffee. He is usually not in a hurry, and he has a favourite route there and back. Listen first of all to how he goes to **Rossio,** and trace his route on the map. You may need to listen several times and / or use the text below.

Sr. Gomes Tomo a Rua do Ouro até à Rua da Conceição. Viro à direita e vou pela Rua da Conceição até à Rua da Prata. Na Rua da Prata volto à esquerda, e vou sempre em frente até à Praça da Figueira. Viro outra vez à esquerda... e estou no Rossio.

à esquerda   em frente   à direita

tomar   *to take*
até a   *until, as far as*
virar   *to turn*
pela   *along the (see note below)*
voltar   *to turn*
vou sempre em frente   *I go straight on*

Note: Like **no, do,** etc., **pela** is another case where two words are combined into one; **pelo = por + o, pela = por + a. Por** has a variety of meanings, but when talking about directions it usually means 'along' or 'through'. For a fuller explanation of how it combines with the word for 'the', consult **Grammar 2.4.**

94

12 Now trace Sr. Gomes's route back to work. If you get it right you will discover the name of a street he doesn't mention. (Answer in **Key.**)

Sr. Gomes Desde o Rossio, tomo a Rua Augusta. Viro na segunda rua à esquerda, a Rua da Assunção, e sigo em frente até ao fim da rua. Depois volto à direita, e vou sempre em frente até chegar à quarta rua transversal, que é a Rua de S. Julião. Viro outra vez à direita e vou pela Rua de S. Julião até chegar à Rua do Ouro e à loja onde trabalho.

desde   *from*
viro na segunda rua   *I turn into the second street*
seguir (sigo)   *to follow (I follow)*
transversal   *that crosses*
depois   *then*

71

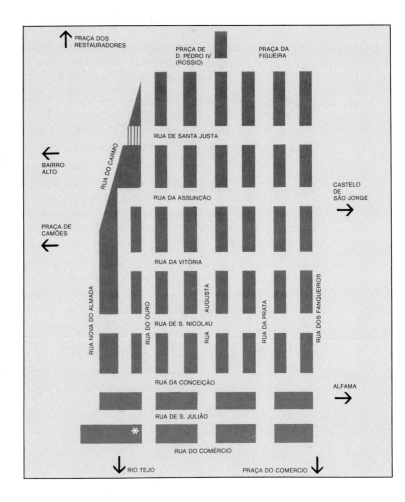

13 You are at the bottom end of **a Rua Augusta,** where it meets **a Rua do Comércio,** and you need to go to **a Rua do Carmo** (top left on the map), via **a Rua de S. Nicolau.**

The following is one possible way you might describe the route you take. Using the map, complete the description by filling in the missing words:

Vou pela Rua Augusta, sempre em frente. Viro na terceira à..............., que é a Rua de S. Nicolau, e sigo até ao............... da rua. No fim da rua, volto à............... e vou sempre em............... até chegar à Rua do Carmo.

Check your answers in the **Key.**

14 When you ask the way in English, the reply is often 'you follow...', 'you turn...', 'you go...', and so on.

Listen to how Pedro is told the way to the nearest bank.

First of all, use the map to follow the directions, and mark with a cross where the bank must be located.

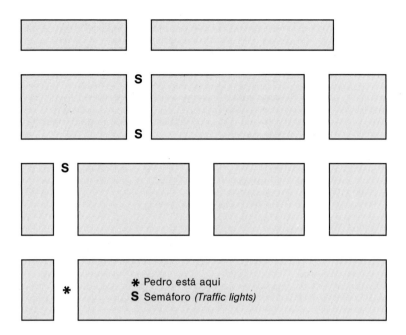

✱ Pedro está aqui
S Semáforo *(Traffic lights)*

Pedro	Desculpe. Há um banco aqui perto?
Transeunte	Bom... Não há muito perto. O mais próximo é o Banco Espírito Santo, que fica na Rua 25 de Abril.
Pedro	E onde é a Rua 25 de Abril?
Transeunte	O senhor vai a pé?
Pedro	Vou.
Transeunte	O senhor segue em frente, até chegar ao semáforo. No semáforo, vira à sua direita e depois vira na primeira à esquerda. No primeiro cruzamento, volta outra vez à direita. Vai sempre em frente, e o banco fica do lado esquerdo, na esquina.
Pedro	Muito obrigado. Bom dia.
Transeunte	De nada. Bom dia.

um cruzamento *a crossroads*
a esquina *the corner*

Consult the **Key** to check Pedro's route and the location of the bank.

95

Now listen again, paying attention particularly to the words for 'follow', 'turn', and 'go'.

Being given instructions:

$$(\text{o senhor, a senhora}) \left\{ \begin{array}{l} \text{vai}\dots \\ \text{toma}\dots \\ \text{vira}\dots \\ \text{volta}\dots \\ \text{segue}\dots \end{array} \right. \quad you \left\{ \begin{array}{l} go\dots \\ take\dots \\ turn\dots \\ turn\dots \\ follow\dots \end{array} \right.$$

73

15 The above form of giving instructions is very common. However, if the instructions are brief, they may be put in a slightly different way.

Listen again to your cassette, and have another look at the map in section 14. In between the second and third set of traffic lights, Pedro realises he hasn't quite taken in the final part of the directions he was given, so he asks the way again.

As you listen, pay particular attention to the words for 'follow', 'turn' and 'go'.

Pedro	Faz favor, minha senhora. Podia-me dizer onde fica o Banco Espírito Santo?
Transeunte	Com certeza. Siga até ao semáforo. Volte à direita e vá sempre em frente. O banco fica do lado esquerdo.
Pedro	Obrigado.
Transeunte	De nada.

This time Pedro is given instructions in a way that is equivalent to saying in English 'Follow...', 'Turn...', 'Go...', as though he were being given commands.

vá... *go...*
tome... *take...*
vire... *turn...*
volte... *turn...*
siga... *follow...*

With many words, the difference between the two ways of giving instructions is very slight (e. g. **volta** and **volte,** or **vira** and **vire**) and may be hardly noticeable when you are listening. With some words, however, the difference is more noticeable (e. g. **segue** and **siga, vai** and **vá**).

If you simply want to be able to understand directions, you needn't learn these differences. However, the 'command' form of giving instructions is used in many other situations — for example, on signs and warnings, in recipes and in instructions on using equipment. If you want more information about the 'command' form of a verb, consult **Grammar 9.10** and **9.11.**

One specific instruction causes confusion both for English-speakers in Portugal, and for Portuguese-speakers in an English-speaking country. **Puxar** is 'to pull', **empurrar** 'to push'. So the instruction 'pull' on a door is **puxe** — pronounced 'push'!

16 You have learned how to ask the way by using **Onde é**...? or **Onde fica**...? These questions will be taken as requests for directions, provided you are referring to somewhere reasonably close at hand: **Onde é a Rua**...? But if you want to find the way to a more distant destination, you need to ask different questions.

In the next two dialogues, concentrate for the moment on the question at the beginning of each — we'll come back in a moment to understanding the replies.

97

Jorge is driving to the Alentejo, and loses his way in Lisbon. Listen to how he asks for the bridge over the Tagus — **a Ponte 25 de Abril.**

Jorge	Desculpe. Para a Ponte 25 de Abril?
Transeunte	Para a Ponte?... O senhor vai por esta rua até ao cruzamento. Volta à sua direita e segue sempre em frente até à rotunda. Na rotunda vira à esquerda e aí vê a indicação para a Ponte.
Jorge	Obrigado.

uma rotunda   *a roundabout*
vê   *you'll see*
a indicação   *the sign*

98

Maria stops her car in the middle of Lisbon to ask the way to Oporto. Notice how she puts her question.

Maria	Faz favor. Qual é o caminho para o Porto?
Transeunte	Para o Porto? Ora bem... A senhora vai por esta avenida, a Avenida da República. Vai sempre em frente. No fim da avenida, passa pelo túnel e vai sair no Campo Grande. Segue o Campo Grande até ao fim e vira à sua direita. A estrada para o Porto está indicada. Não tem problema.
Maria	Portanto, vou sempre em frente até ao fim do Campo Grande, e viro à direita?
Transeunte	Exactamente, minha senhora.
Maria	Muito obrigada.

o caminho   *the way*
Ora bem...   *Well now...*
sair   *to go out*

> To ask which is the way to...:
>
> **Para...?**
> **Qual é o caminho para...?**
>
> **Para...?** can be used for both distant and nearby destinations.

97-98

17   If you would like more listening practice, go back to the previous two dialogues.

In the directions given to Jorge, how many right turns are there? And how many left turns? (Answer in **Key.**)

The route Maria is given involves only one turn — is it right or left? (Answer in **Key.**)

18   Directions are not always easy to understand, even in your own language. So it's useful to be able to ask someone to say it again, or to speak more slowly. You are already familiar with most of the words you need for this.

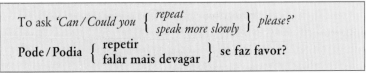

> To ask 'Can / Could you { *repeat* / *speak more slowly* } *please?*'
>
> **Pode / Podia** { **repetir** / **falar mais devagar** } **se faz favor?**

75

Finding a room

The next sections give you an opportunity to revise some of the skills you have learned in the course so far, by applying them to a particular situation — arriving at a hotel.

You already know how to ask the essential questions and how to select what you want:

Tem...?   Onde...?
Há...?   A que horas...?
Quanto é...?   Queria...
Qual é...?

What you need now are some new words to complete these opening phrases. In the following dialogues, you are asked to pick out some of the essential words you will need. Don't worry if at first you don't understand the entire conversation.

19 The first thing you would want to establish is whether a room (**um quarto**) is available.

In this dialogue between José and the receptionist (**a empregada da recepção**), identify the words for 'vacant', 'vacancy' and 'occupied'. Then consult the **Key** to check your answers.

José	Boa tarde.
Recepção	Boa tarde.
José	Têm quartos vagos?
Recepção	Lamento, mas não temos vagas. Todos os quartos estão ocupados.
José	Há outro hotel aqui perto?
Recepção	Sim, senhor. Há outro no fim desta rua.
José	Obrigado.
Recepção	De nada. Boa tarde.

lamento   *I'm sorry*
todos   *all*

20 After you have checked your answer in the Key, listen to the dialogue once more. Where is the other hotel? (Answer in **Key**.)

21 Rosa is enquiring on behalf of her family, and needs two rooms.

Can you pick out the words for 'a single room', and two ways of saying 'a double room'? (Answer in **Key**.)

Rosa	Boa tarde. Têm quartos vagos?
Recepção	Temos, sim. Para quantas pessoas?
Rosa	Somos três. Queria um quarto simples e um duplo.
Recepção	Pode ser o 17 e o 23.
Rosa	Qual é o preço, por favor?
Recepção	O quarto simples são dois mil e oitocentos escudos, e o quarto de casal três mil e trezentos.
Rosa	Está bem. A que horas é o pequeno almoço?
Recepção	Entre as 7.00 e as 9.30.
Rosa	E onde é que se toma?
Recepção	Aqui em baixo, no restaurante. Faz favor, não se importa de assinar?
Rosa	Com certeza.

o preço   *the price, the cost*
o pequeno almoço   *breakfast*
onde (é que) se toma?   *where does one have it?*
aqui em baixo   *down here*
não se importa de…?   *would you mind…?*
assinar   *to sign*

22 Check your answer, and then listen again. How much is the single room? And the double? (Answer in **Key**.)

23 Filipe chooses a room with its own bathroom. What are the words for bath and bathroom? (Answer in **Key**.)

Filipe	Boa tarde. Há um quarto simples disponível?
Recepção	Quantas noites vai ficar?
Filipe	É para hoje e amanhã.
Recepção	Portanto, duas noites… Quer com casa de banho privativa?
Filipe	Quanto custa?
Recepção	São três mil escudos.
Filipe	Então com banho, se faz favor.
Recepção	Pronto. É o 106. Aqui tem as chaves. O senhor toma o elevador e sobe ao terceiro andar. O quarto fica à direita, ao fundo do corredor.
Filipe	Muito obrigado.
Recepção	De nada. Boa estadia.

disponível   *available*
Quanto custa?   *How much does it cost?*
uma chave   *a key*
o elevador   *the lift*
o terceiro andar   *the third floor*
Boa estadia   *Enjoy your stay*

24 Check your answer, and then listen again. Which direction is Filipe's room, as he comes out of the lift? (Answer in **Key**.)

To ask for a room:

Tem { quartos vagos? / um quarto disponível? }   *Have you (got)* { *any rooms free? / a room available?* }

Queria um quarto { simples / duplo / de casal }   *I'd like a* { *single / double* } *room*

Qual é o preço? / Quanto é? / Quanto custa? }   *How much is it?*

com / sem } banho   *with / without* } *a bathroom*

Onde { fica / é } { o quarto? / a casa de banho? / o elevador? / o bar? }   *Where is the* { *room? / bathroom / toilet? / lift? / bar?* }

25 Now book yourself into a hotel. You want a double room, with bath, for five nights. Complete the following dialogue by putting one appropriate word in each gap.

Recepção Boa noite.

Você Boa noite. Têm quartos ....?

Recepção Temos, sim. Simples ou de ....?

Você De..............., se faz favor.

Recepção Quer.............. de banho privativa?

Você Qual é o.............. com banho?

Recepção .... quatro mil e duzentos escudos.

Você Então, um quarto com banho, por favor.

Recepção É só para esta noite?

Você Não, é para.............. noites.

Recepção Está bem. Então é o número 57. Aqui tem.............. chaves.

Você Obrigado. Onde.............. o quarto?

Recepção É no quinto...............

Você No quinto!.............. elevador?

Recepção Elevador?.............. certeza! Fica ali à direita,.............. lado do restaurante.

Você A que horas é o.............. almoço?

Recepção Das 7.00 até às 10.00.

Você ....

Recepção De nada. Boa noite.

Now check your answers on the cassette and / or in the **Key**.

Resumo

To ask { 'Is there a…?':   Há um(a)…?
 'Are there any…?':   Há…?

To ask where a place is, or something which has a permanent location:

Onde { é…?
 fica?

To ask if it's { far: <br> near: É/Fica { longe?
 perto?

To ask where a person is (or anything that moves or can be moved):   **Onde está…?**

Being given directions:

vai…	vá…
toma…	tome…
vira…	vire…
volta…	volte…
segue…	siga…
sobe…	suba…

To ask the way to…: { **Para…, se faz favor?**
 Qual é o caminho para…?

Asking 'Could you { speak more slowly?': <br> repeat?':

     Podia { **falar mais devagar?**
 repetir?

To say you're staying… nights: **Fico**
 Ficamos } **… noites.**

Vocabulário

aqui	virar	um quarto { simples
ali	voltar	duplo/de casal
perto	seguir	vago
longe	o caminho	disponível
atrás (de)	uma vila	uma vaga
em frente (de)	uma estrada	o preço
em baixo	uma rua	a chave
entre	uma avenida	o elevador
no fim (de)	uma praça	o andar
ao fundo (de)	um largo	a casa de banho
no meio (de)	uma rotunda	o pequeno almoço
ao lado (de)	um cruzamento	um banco
desde	o semáforo	o correio
depois	o próximo	uma farmácia
ir { à esquerda	o mais próximo	uma igreja
em frente		
à direita	um hotel	hoje
	uma pensão	amanhã

79

Mais alguma coisa?

103

As an introduction to the Alentejo, listen on your cassette to a song performed by an amateur male-voice choir from Reguengos de Monsaraz, that we recorded during the preparation of the *Discovering Portuguese* television programmes. Reguengos de Monsaraz is a small town near the River Guadiana, some 30 miles from Évora, and the song is about leaving home. The simple, precise words recall the Portuguese tradition of oral poetry.

Since a translation is provided, the unfamiliar words here are not included in the Glossary.

Linda vila vou deixar	*Lovely town I'm going to leave*
Mas custa-me a partida	*But it's hard for me to depart*
Levo no peito a chorar	*I bear in my breast weeping*
A minha alma entristecida	*My saddened soul*
Reguengos de Monsaraz	*Reguengos de Monsaraz*
És minha terra natal	*You're my native land*
Deixar-te não sou capaz	*I cannot leave you*
És jardim em Portugal	*You're a garden in Portugal*
És jardim em Portugal	*You're a garden in Portugal*
Regado pelo Guadiana	*Watered by the Guadiana*
Diz o jardineiro cantando	*Says the gardener in his song*
Linda vila alentejana	*Lovely Alentejan town*
Com os teus lindos trigais	*With your lovely wheat-fields*
Ondeando como o mar	*Rippling like the sea*
Dez vinhedos e olivais	*Ten vineyards and olive groves*
És concelho de encantar	*You're a place of delight*
Tudo em ti é natural	*Everything in you is natural*
E de tudo és capaz	*And you're able to do everything*
És minha terra natal	*You're my native land*
Reguengos de Monsaraz	*Reguengos de Monsaraz*

Um concelho is a 'council', a sub-division of a district for administration purposes in Portugal.

Alentejo: the cork harvest

O Alentejo

A Ponte 25 de Abril links Lisbon to the industrial towns on the far bank of the Tagus, and to the road southwards to the Alentejo — **além Tejo** (beyond the Tagus). This province, the largest in Portugal (almost a third of the country), is very different from the provinces of the North. In the North, you find mountains and lush green valleys, scattered with granite houses and villages, and a religious, conservative people whose remote ancestors were Celtic and Germanic.

In contrast, the Alentejo belongs to the Mediterranean. It is an immense, arid, rolling plain, stretching to the horizon, broken here and there by plantations of cork oak (**o sobreiro**) or holm-oak (**a azinheira**), and by white towns spreading over distant hill-tops. Here the cultural heritage is Roman and Arab. The main products are wheat (**o trigo**) — the Alentejo is the granary of Portugal — olives (**as azeitonas**), and cork (**a cortiça**).

Alentejan farm worker

But the most important difference between North and South lies in the system of land-ownership. As we said in Unit 3, the land problem in the North is its division into individual holdings too small to be viable — **minifúndios.** The situation inherited by the Alentejo is the reverse — the existence of vast estates (**latifúndios**) owned by a few families — a system dating originally from the Christian 'reconquest' from the Arabs. The result of this concentration of land in the hands of a few owners is that the majority of the rural population are labourers with no land of their own, who have suffered the experience of seasonal employment only, at sowing and harvest times. They have a strong sense of solidarity with each other, and of grievance against the landowners, feelings which are often expressed in their singing — Alentejo choirs, though not to everyone's taste, are an experience not to be missed. Not surprisingly, the **Partido Comunista Português,** founded in the 1920s, has had its strongest support in the districts of Setúbal, Évora and Beja.

Alentejan landscape

O 25 de Abril

Appropriately, a protest song in the Alentejan vocal idiom was
broadcast on the night of 24 April 1974 as part of the signal for the
military revolt. The song was José Afonso's **Grândola, vila morena.**
It begins (roughly translated) as follows:

Grândola vila morena	*Grândola dark-skinned town*
Terra da fraternidade	*Land of fraternity*
O povo é quem mais ordena	*It's ordinary people who make the decisions*
Dentro de ti ó cidade	*In the city of Grândola*

(**Moreno** also suggests 'Moorish' — the Arab past. This song was
banned under the Caetano regime.)

In the early hours of 25 April, a group of young military officers —
o Movimento das Forças Armadas — began what was to be a virtually
bloodless uprising. Within 24 hours western Europe's oldest
dictatorship had surrendered. In the months and years following April
1974, land reform in the Alentejo, **a reforma agrária,** became a central
political issue, and one that tended to divide the revolutionary South
from the conservative small-holders of the North. Many of the large
estates in the Alentejo were occupied by the workers and turned into
cooperative farms. Eventually a series of new laws attempted to find
a compromise between the interests of the original owners and those
of the workers.

But the significance of **o 25 de Abril** goes far beyond the problems of the Alentejo. Within Portugal, the coup had immediate popular support. The first consequences were the release of the political prisoners of the Caetano regime, the return of the many exiles — including the present president, Mário Soares — the abolition of censorship and of the hated secret police — the PIDE. The collapse of the 48 year-old dictatorship also unleashed pent-up creative energies, and in the months that followed every aspect of the organisation of society was questioned in endless meetings and debates. Since, in 1974, no-one under the age of 70 in Portugal had any experience of free elections, it is not surprising that the transition to democracy was at times a chaotic and bitterly divisive process. Out of the turmoil, however, Portugal has emerged with a new sense of social justice. The process that began on 25 April 1974 has culminated in Portugal's integration into Europe as a member of the EEC in January 1986.

Beyond Portugal too, **o 25 de Abril** has had far-reaching consequences. A major part of the original motivation of the military was frustration at the Caetano regime's unwillingness to negotiate a settlement of the colonial wars in Africa. Portugal's final withdrawal, in 1974 and 1975, from its former African colonies brought to an end 500 years of empire, and radically changed the political map of southern Africa.

O 25 de Abril: the Carmo barracks, Lisbon, scene of Caetano's surrender

5 VAMOS ÀS COMPRAS

Unit 5 deals primarily with shopping situations, but much of the language that follows is useful in other situations too. In fact, you already have some of the basic skills you will need when shopping: being able to use **Tem**…?, **Há**…?, **Queria**… and so on. So this unit gives you a chance to revise these skills and to build on what you know already. It covers such aspects as saying what you need, specifying quantity, size or colour, and asking if you can do something (e.g. change money, or try on an item of clothing).

Is there any left?

1   In the following two dialogues, people discover they have run out of various items they need. You know how to ask 'Is there a…?' or 'Are there any…?' Now listen first to how to say 'Is there still some… left?' and 'There isn't any… left'. Don't worry if you don't understand everything to begin with — we'll come back to other parts of these dialogues in a moment.

Jaime and Celeste plan to have dinner at home… but it's Sunday and there isn't much food left.

Celeste	Jantamos hoje em casa?
Jaime	Está bem. O que há?
Celeste	Bom… Hoje é domingo. Já não há muito!
Jaime	Ainda há carne?
Celeste	Não, já não há. Tenho de ir amanhã ao talho.
Jaime	Mas há ovos. Podemos fazer uma omeleta.

Marta offers her visitor a ham sandwich and then discovers she has run out of bread (**o pão**).

Marta	Quer lanchar? Vou preparar um chá e umas sanduíches de fiambre.
Inês	Óptimo. Estou com fome!

Momentos depois…

Marta	Desculpe. Já não há pão. Tenho de ir à padaria.
Inês	Olhe, porque não lanchamos na pastelaria?

óptimo *splendid*
com fome *hungry*
olhe *look*

To ask { 'Is there still some…?' 'Is there any… left?' } **Ainda há…?**

To say { 'There's still some…': **Ainda há…** 'There's none left': **Já não há**

Ainda há pão?	*Is there still some bread?*
Já não há pão	*There's no bread left*
Já não há	*There's none left*

'I have to…'

2   Listen again to the previous two dialogues on your cassette, and then carry on to the next one. This time listen particularly to how people say 'I/We have to go to the…'.

104

In the first, Jaime and Celeste have run out of meat, and Celeste has to go to the butcher's (**o talho**).

105

In the second, Marta has run out of bread and has to go to the baker's (**a padaria**).

106

In the next dialogue, Luís and Margarida have almost nothing left for lunch — and they have run out of money.

Luís	Tenho de ir às compras antes do almoço. Já não há nada no frigorífico.
Margarida	Mas não temos dinheiro. Temos de ir primeiro ao banco. Que horas são?
Luís	É meio-dia e um quarto. O banco está fechado. Fecha às 11.45.
Margarida	E só abre à uma. Então, paciência! Temos de esperar.

ir às compras   *to go shopping*
fecha   *it closes*
abre   *it opens*
esperar   *to wait*

To say you have to do something, use:

Tenho
Temos } **de**…

and add the word for the action.

Tenho de ir para casa   *I have to go home*
Temos de ir ao talho   *We have to go to the butcher's*

O horário dos bancos

3   Os bancos em Portugal abrem às 8.30 e fecham às 14.45.

But what time do they close for lunch?...............
And what time do they re-open after lunch?..............

106

Listen again to the previous item on your cassette, and check the answers in the **Key**.

Names of shops

4   Often the word for a particular kind of shop or other business is based on the word for what it sells (or for its speciality), with the ending **-aria**: **pastel — pastelaria; cerveja — cervejaria**. This is not always the case, e.g. the shops illustrated on page 86, **a padaria, o talho**.

Now try experimenting with words that you know already, or ones that have cropped up so far in this unit.

85

(left) o talho
(right) a padaria

If you arrived at each of the following shops at closing time, and the shelves were apparently empty, how would you say 'Please, is there any... left?'?

1. a frutaria   3. a peixaria
2. o talho   4. a padaria

Check your answers in the **Key.**

'I need a...' 'I need to...'

5 In the next two dialogues, two couples are planning their shopping. Listen to how they say what they need, and where they need to go.

Helena is going to do the shopping, but Francisco (helpfully!) offers to make a list — **faço uma lista.**

Helena	Então, vou às compras?
Francisco	Está bem. Eu faço uma lista.
Helena	Precisamos de arroz, feijão e café. Mais alguma coisa?
Francisco	Ainda há pão?
Helena	Tens razão! Já não há. Portanto... feijão, arroz, café e pão. Só preciso de ir à mercearia — e à padaria.

Tens razão! *You're right!* (**Tens** is the more intimate **tu** form of **tem**.)
a mercearia *the grocer's*

Maria	Vamos fazer uma caldeirada para o jantar?
Carlos	Boa ideia. Mas temos de comprar os ingredientes. De que precisamos?
Maria	Preciso de comprar peixe e marisco. Os outros ingredientes já temos.
Carlos	Vamos à peixaria, então?
Maria	Ou ao supermercado.

> To say *'I / We need…'*, use:
>
> **Preciso**
> **Precisamos** } de…
>
> and add the words for the things you need, e.g.
>
> **Preciso de calças novas** *I need new trousers*
> **Precisamos dum guia** *We need a guide-book*
>
> To say *'I / We need to…'*, use:
>
> **Preciso**
> **Precisamos** } de…
>
> and add the word for the action, e.g.
>
> **Preciso de comprar sapatos** *I need to buy shoes*
> **Precisamos de ir ao mercado** *We need to go to the market*

6   Complete each of the following by writing an appropriate phrase in Portuguese for 'I'll / We'll have to go to the…'. For example, the answer to no. 1 is **Temos de ir à frutaria.**

In two cases **eu** and **nós** are given in brackets to show that the answers are intended to be 'I' and 'we'. In all the other cases it should be clear whether 'I' or 'we' is required.

1.   Precisamos de fruta. ....
2.   Preciso de comprar peixe. ....
3.   Já não há carne. (Eu) ....
4.   Precisamos de comprar pão. ....
5.   Já não há café. (Nós) ....
6.   Preciso de aspirina. (*aspirin*) ....
7.   Precisamos de comprar pastéis. ....

Now check your answers on the cassette and / or in the **Key.**

109

'(Where) Can I…?'

7 You learned in Unit 2 how to ask 'May I?' – **Posso?** But you will also
need to combine **posso** with other words, so that you can ask, for
example, if or where you can buy a particular thing. In the next two
dialogues listen to how people ask 'Where can I/we…?'.

110

João stops someone in the street to ask where he can buy postcards
(a postcard is **um postal**).

João	Desculpe. Onde é que posso comprar postais?
Transeunte	Postais? Talvez na papelaria.
João	E onde é a papelaria?
Transeunte	É muito perto. O senhor segue por aqui e vira na segunda à direita. Vê logo a papelaria, do lado esquerdo.
João	Muito obrigado.
Transeunte	De nada.

uma papelaria   *a stationer's*
logo   *immediately*

111

Filipe and Ester want to buy stamps (a stamp is **um selo**).

Filipe	Faz favor. Onde podemos comprar selos?
Transeunte	No correio, aí em frente da estação. Mas não sei se ainda está aberto a estas horas.

sei   *I know*

> To ask if (where) you may / can do something, use:
>
> (Onde) $\left\{ \begin{array}{l} \textbf{posso}…? \\ \textbf{podemos}…? \end{array} \right.$
>
> and add the word for the action, e.g.
>
> **Posso alugar um carro?**   *Can I hire a car?*
> **Podemos ficar duas noites?**   *May we stay two nights?*
> **Onde posso comprar pão?**   *Where can I buy bread?*

88

■ CÂMBIOS NACIONAIS E ESTRANGEIROS

Moedas e notas

Lisboa 27.1.87

	(por unidade) Compra	Vende
Rand — África do Sul	50$20	56$20
Marco	76$35	77$55
Xelim — Áustria	10$80	11$00
Franco — Bélgica	3$476	3$726
Cruzado — Brasil	3$800	6$300
Dólar — Canadá (notas de 1 e 2)	102$90	105$40
Dólar — Canadá (notas maiores)	103$40	105$90
Coroa — Dinamarca	20$15	20$55
Peseta — Espanha	1$052	1$172
Dólar — E. U. A. (notas de 1 e 2)	139$30	142$80
(notas de 5 a 1000)	139$80	143$30
Markka — Finlândia	30$50	31$10
Franco — França	22$90	23$60
Florim — Holanda	67$70	68$80
Libra — Irlanda	203$75	207$75
Lira — Itália	$098	$113
Iene — Japão	$869	$924
Coroa — Noruega	19$70	20$20
Libra — Inglaterra	213$25	217$75
Coroa — Suécia	21$35	21$85
Franco — Suíça	91$30	92$80
Bolívar — Venezuela	5$75	6$75

OBS. Estas cotações devem ser consideradas a título informativo. Todas as operações estão sujeitas a imposto de 6 1000.

Banco de Portugal 27.1.87

CHEQUES E ORDENS DE PAGAMENTO		COMPRA	VENDA
E. U. A.	USD	140$388	140$820
Grã-Bretanha	GBP	214$485	215$063
Alemanha (R. Fed.)	DEM	77$202	77$350
África do Sul	ZAR	67$956	68$134
Áustria	ATS	10$976	10$998
Bélgica	BEC	3$723 9	3$731 3
Canadá	CAD	103$990	104$304
Dinamarca	DKK	20$309	20$351
Espanha	ESP	1$092 5	1$095 1
Finlândia	FIM	30$789	30$859
França	FRF	23$123	23$171
Grécia	GRD	1$056 6	1$059 2
Holanda	NLG	68$498	68$630
Irlanda	IEP	204$817	205$281
Itália	ITL	$108 59	$108 81
Japão	JPY	$923 23	$925 01
Noruega	NOK	19$932	19$982
Suécia	SEK	21$570	21$620
Suíça	CHF	92$019	92$199
UN. conta da CEE	XEU	159$072	159$562

Posso cambiar um cheque?

8 A situation in which you might well want to ask a question beginning **Posso…?** is when changing money in a bank. This situation involves skills you already have, but you will need some new vocabulary.

Sr. Pinto has returned from the USA for a holiday. One of the first things he needs to do is change money. Listen out for the two words which mean 'to change'. (Answer in **Key.**)

Sr. Pinto	Boa tarde. Posso trocar dólares?
Empregada	Com certeza.
Sr. Pinto	Qual é a cotação do dólar?
Empregada	A compra é a 148$00 e a venda é a 149$00.
Sr. Pinto	Então queria cambiar 300 dólares, por favor.
Empregada	Tem o seu passaporte, se faz favor?… Qual é a sua morada aqui em Lisboa?
Sr. Pinto	Rua Manuel Ferreira de Andrade, 187, 3.°-Dto.
Empregada	Não se importa de assinar aqui?
Sr. Pinto	Com certeza.
Empregada	Pronto. Aqui está o seu passaporte.

a cotação   *the rate*
a compra   *the buying rate*
a venda   *the selling rate*

9 Now for some revision of the words for numbers. Listen again to the previous dialogue, and write down in words the numbers needed to answer the following questions.

1. What is the rate at which dollars are bought?
2. And the rate at which they are sold?
3. How many dollars does Sr. Pinto change?
4. What is the number of his Lisbon house?

Check your answers in the **Key.**

10 Sra. Smith has recently arrived from London and needs to change a Eurocheque. Despite her perfect Portuguese, the bank clerk assumes she is not familiar with Portuguese banks: he gives her **uma chapa** (a small disk with a number) and explains that she must take it to the cashier's desk (**a caixa**) in order to be paid her **escudos**.

Is the cashier on Sra. Smith's right, or on her left? (Answer in **Key**.)

Sra. Smith	Faz favor. Onde posso cambiar um eurocheque?
Empregado	No balcão ao fundo à direita.

Momentos depois...

Sra. Smith	Boa tarde. Queria trocar um eurocheque de cem libras.
Empregado	Sim senhora. Tem o seu cartão?
Sra. Smith	Tenho.
Empregado	E o seu passaporte?... Qual é a sua morada?
Sra. Smith	Estou no Hotel Fénix, Praça Marquês de Pombal, 8.

Minutos mais tarde...

Empregado	Já está. A senhora tem de entregar esta chapa na caixa para receber o dinheiro.
Sra. Smith	Já sei. Mas onde é a caixa?
Empregado	É à sua esquerda, ao fundo, aí onde está a bicha.
Sra. Smith	Obrigada.

o balcão   *the counter*
um cartão   *a cheque card*
entregar   *to hand over*
receber   *to receive*
a bicha   *the queue*

11 Now try some practice. You're staying at the Hotel Fénix. It's 11.00 a.m. and you have gone into a bank to cash a cheque.

Empregado	....
Você	*(Greet him and ask if you can change a cheque for £50.)*
	....
Empregado	(1) *(What is he asking you for?)*
	....
Você	*(Say 'Yes, I have'.)*
	....
Empregado	(2) *(What is he asking you to do?)*
	(3) *(What information is he asking for?)*
	....
Você	*(Answer him. Begin* **Estou**...*)*
	....
Empregado	(4) *(What is he telling you to do?)*
	....
Você	*(Thank him.)*
	....

Check your answers in the **Key.**

12 In the right-hand column below are possible answers to the questions in the left-hand column. But the order of the answers has been jumbled. Number each answer to show which question it belongs to.

Perguntas	Respostas
(1) Onde posso comprar carne?	( ) No correio, que fica aqui na praça.
(2) Posso cambiar dinheiro no hotel?	( ) Não, não temos. A senhora tem de ir à mercearia.
(3) Qual é a cotação da libra?	( ) Rua 25 de Abril, 7, 2.º-Esq. (sete, segundo, esquerdo)
(4) Onde é que podemos comprar pão?	( ) Há um talho no Centro Comercial.
(5) Faz favor. Tem arroz?	( ) Não, não pode. Tem de ir ao banco.
(6) Qual é a sua morada?	( ) Talvez nesta livraria, aqui em frente.
(7) Onde podemos comprar selos?	( ) A padaria mais próxima é no fim daquela rua.
(8) Faz favor, onde posso comprar um guia de Portugal?	( ) A compra é a duzentos e doze escudos.

Check your answers in the **Key**.

'How much is / are the...?'

13 You already know how to ask how much something is by using **Quanto é...?** However, with goods that are priced by weight (e.g. so much a kilo), there is another way of asking the price.

Miguel has gone to the supermarket to buy **presunto** and **chouriço**. Listen particularly to how he asks the price in each case, and for how the assistant replies.

First he has to find the right part of the shop.

Miguel	Faz favor. Onde é a charcutaria?
Empregada	É lá ao fundo, ao lado do talho.
Miguel	Obrigado.

Momentos depois...

Miguel	Boa tarde. A como é o presunto?
Empregado	É a 1314$00 o quilo.
Miguel	Queria duzentos gramas, faz favor.
Empregado	E que mais?
Miguel	A como são os chouriços?
Empregado	Este é a 525$00 e aquele é à 1130$00. É muito bom — é chouriço caseiro da Serra da Estrela.
Miguel	Então levo meio quilo daquele.
Empregado	Mais alguma coisa?
Miguel	Mais nada, obrigado.

a charcutaria   *the delicatessen*
um quilo   *a kilo*
um grama   *a gram*
caseiro   *home-made*
levo   *I'll take*

> To ask the price of something sold by weight:
>
> **A como** { **é...**
>   { **são...**
>
> **A como é o queijo?**   *How much is the cheese?*
> **A como são as laranjas?**   *How much are the oranges?*

14   If you would like some more revision of numbers, try writing in words the prices of the **presunto** and of the **chouriços** in the above dialogue. You may need to listen again to the cassette.

Check your answers in the **Key.**

Saying how much you want

116

15   João has just finished shopping in the supermarket, and has reached the check-out (**a caixa**). As the **empregada** checks out each item she reads the price on it.

Below is a list of what João has bought. Listen to your cassette and write in figures the cost of each item, and the total cost.

Empregada   2 quilos de batatas...............
             1 pacote de café...............
             Meia dúzia de ovos...............
             1 litro de leite...............
             250 gramas de manteiga...............
             1 lata de azeite...............
             1 caixa de marmelada...............
             1 frasco de mel...............
João   Quanto é?
Empregada   São...............

um pacote   *a packet*
uma dúzia   *a dozen*
um litro   *a litre*
uma lata   *a tin, a can*
o azeite   *olive oil*
uma caixa   *a box*
a marmelada   *quince preserve*
um frasco   *a pot*
o mel   *honey*

117

16   Alice too has just reached the **caixa.** Here is her shopping list. Listen to the **empregada** on your cassette and fill in the missing words on the list (words for quantities, and for various kinds of container). Then check your answer in the **Key.**

Empregada	Meio .... de uvas	40$00
	Duas .... de vinho tinto	570$00
	Um .... de óleo	200$00
	Uma .... de ovos	160$00
	Um .... de açúcar	96$50
	Um .... de doce de laranja	175$00

Alice	Quanto é?
Empregada	São 1241$50.
Alice	Tem troco de 5000$00?
Empregada	Tenho. Arranja-me quinze tostões, se faz favor?
Alice	Acho que sim.
Empregada	Faz favor — o troco.
Alice	Obrigada.

o óleo   *cooking oil*
o doce de laranja   *marmalade*
o troco   *change*
Tem troco de…?   *Have you got change for…?*
Arranja-me…?   *Have you got…?* (literally *'Can you arrange… for me?'*)

O escudo

17   The Portuguese unit of currency, **o escudo**, is divided into
100 **centavos** — in theory, at least. In practice, however, the only
coin below **um escudo** that is still in use is 50 **centavos**, and this
has become such a trivial sum that the coin is unlikely to survive
much longer.

As you will have noticed from prices that have cropped up in the course, the **escudo** symbol $ is placed after the number of **escudos**, and is followed by two zeros or by the number of **centavos**, e.g. 2$50 (two **escudos** fifty **centavos**), 250$00 (two hundred and fifty **escudos**).

When you are dealing with small change, you may come across **um tostão** — an old word for a small coin. It is the equivalent of 10 **centavos**, and you will sometimes hear people say **cinco tostões** (i.e. 50 **centavos**), **dez tostões** (1 **escudo**) or **quinze tostões** (1$50). Perhaps more important, if only for the sum involved, is **um conto**. This is another way of saying **mil escudos**. It is used very commonly, and particularly to refer to very large sums, e.g. **mil contos** (i.e. 1 000 000$00).

18 You are shopping in a village which hasn't got a supermarket, so you need to go to the grocer's. Here is your shopping list:

1 kilo rice
1/2 kilo coffee
1 pkt. butter
1/2 litre olive oil
1 box quince preserve
1 kilo sugar

Your cassette gives you one side of the dialogue below. Listen and speak your part. You may want to rehearse a bit before you begin.

First you need to ask your way. You stop a woman in the street (remember to say 'excuse me') and ask if there is a grocer's nearby.

Você	....
Transeunte	Há uma na praça. Vá por esta rua, sempre em frente. Fica perto.
Você	....
Transeunte	De nada.

You find the grocer's and go in...

Merceeiro	Boa tarde. Que deseja?
Você	*(Greet him and ask for the first two items on your list.)*
	....
Merceeiro	E que mais?
Você	*(Tell him the next two items on your list.)*
	....
Merceeiro	Mais alguma coisa?
Você	*(Say you would also like... the final two items on your list.)*
	....
Merceeiro	E que mais?
Você	*(Tell him that's all thank you, and ask how much it is.)*
	....
Merceeiro	São 1955$00.
Você	*(Ask him if he has change for 5000$00.)*
	....
Merceeiro	Tenho. Faz favor. *(He hands you your change.)*
Você	*(Thank him.)*
	....
Merceeiro	Obrigado eu. Muito boa tarde.

118

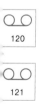
To check this dialogue, carry on with your cassette. Then, if you want further practice, try writing your part of the dialogue, and check what you have written in the **Key**.

'May I have a look?'

19 You have learned how to combine **posso** with words for actions — for example: **Posso cambiar um cheque?** Apart from banking, another situation in which you might need to use **Posso...?** is when choosing something to buy: 'May I have a look at...?'.

Sofia is shopping for a cotton dress (**um vestido de algodão**) in a boutique in the Centro Comercial. Listen first of all to how she asks to have a look. Don't worry if you can't follow all the dialogue — we'll deal with other parts of it in a moment.

Sofia	Bom dia. Posso ver um vestido de algodão?
Empregada	Temos vários modelos. Gosta deste?
Sofia	Gosto do modelo, mas não gosto muito da cor.
Empregada	Temo-los noutras cores. Azul por exemplo, ou encarnado.
Sofia	Gosto do azul. Posso prová-lo?
Empregada	Qual é o seu número?
Sofia	É o 36.

a cor   *the colour*
noutro   (**em + outro**) *in another*
azul   *blue*
encarnado   *red*

> Asking to have a look:
>
> In English we say, for example, *'Can I have a look at some cotton dresses?'* Notice that in Portuguese you say *'Can I see a...?'*
>
> **Posso ver um vestido de algodão?**

'May I try it on?'

20 Listen again to the previous dialogue. After some discussion of colour, Sofia says she likes the blue dress. This time listen particularly to how she asks if she may try it on.

In the same shop Helena is looking for a silk blouse (**uma blusa de seda**). Once again, listen particularly to how she asks if she may try on the one she selects.

Empregada	Bom dia. Quer ajuda?
Helena	Queria ver uma blusa de seda, por favor.
Empregada	Temo-las de várias cores — brancas, azuis, cinzentas, castanhas. Tem alguma preferência?
Helena	Gosto desta castanha. Posso experimentá-la?
Empregada	Com certeza. Qual é o seu número?
Helena	É o 34.

95

a ajuda *help*
cinzento *grey*
castanho *brown*

> To ask if you may try something on:
>
> Posso { prová-lo?
>   prová-la?
>   experimentá-lo?
>   experimentá-la?

Note: -lo / -la

21 When the words for 'it' (**o, a**) or 'them' (**os, as**) come at the end of a word ending in **r** or **s,** the sound and spelling change:

O vinho é bom? Posso prová-lo?	*Is the wine good?*
(NOT **provar-o**)	*May I try it.*
Gosto desta saia. Posso experimentá-la?	*I like this skirt.*
(NOT **experimentar-a**)	*May I try it on?*
Temo-las em várias cores.	*We have them in several*
(NOT **temos-as**)	*colours.*

For further examples see **Grammar 7.6.**

Note that you can also use **provar** for 'to try' or 'to taste' food and drink.

122

22 Now try some practice. First have another look at the various words for colours and items of clothing that have cropped up so far. You will also need two new words for clothes: **uma camisola** (a pullover) and **um fato** (a suit).

You are being asked by the shop assistant if you like particular items. First of all, listen to your cassette without replying to the assistant's questions. Instead, answer in English the questions below.

The following items are mentioned — but not necessarily in this order. What colour is

1. the blouse:............................? 4. the dress:...............................?
2. the jacket:............................? 5. the skirt:................................?
3. the pullover:.......................? 6. the suit:.................................?

Check your answers in the **Key.**

122

23 Now listen again and reply to the shop assistant's questions. Each time, answer 'Yes, I do' and ask if you may try it on (use **provar**).

Check your answers on the cassette and / or in the **Key.**

123

'It suits me'

24 You have already come across the word **ficar**, used when asking where something is (**Onde fica...?**), or meaning 'to stay' (**Ficamos duas noites**). Here is yet another use of **ficar**.

Helena and Sofia are still choosing clothes. Listen particularly to how they say something suits them, or doesn't suit them.

Helena	Afinal a blusa castanha não me fica bem. Posso experimentar a branca?
Empregada	Pode, sim.

Minutos mais tarde…

Helena	Esta fica-me bastante bem. Quanto é?
Empregada	São doze contos.
Helena	Não é nada cara. Levo-a.

afinal   *in the end, as it turns out*
bastante   *quite*
nada caro   *not at all expensive*
levo-a   *I'll take it*

Sofia	Gosto do vestido azul, mas está um pouco apertado.
Empregada	Então experimente o número acima.

Minutos mais tarde…

Empregada	Fica-lhe muito bem. Que acha?
Sofia	Sim, fica-me bem. Quanto é?
Empregada	São três mil e quinhentos escudos.
Sofia	Está bem. Então levo este.

apertado   *tight*
o número acima   *the next size up*
Que acha?   *What do you think?*

To say {	'It suits me':	**Fica-me** }	**bem**
	'It suits you':	**Fica-lhe**	
To say {	'It doesn't suit me':	**Não me fica** }	**bem**
	'It doesn't suit you':	**Não lhe fica**	

You may have noticed that the words for 'me', 'it', 'them' etc. sometimes follow the verb and sometimes come before it. It is simplest if you assume that they usually come after the verb, except in certain circumstances — e.g. when the statement begins with **não**, as above: **não me fica bem**. For a full explanation, see **Grammar 7.5**.

25   Now try buying a woollen pullover — **uma camisola de lã**. The assistant's words are on the cassette. Speak your part of the dialogue. You may want to rehearse what you are going to say before you begin.

Empregada	Boa tarde. Quer ajuda?
Você	*(Greet her, and say you would like to have a look at some woollen pullovers, please.)*

....

Empregada	Uma camisola de lã? Temo-las em várias cores. Tem preferência de cor? Faz favor de ver.
Você	*(Tell her you like the grey one. Ask her if you may try it on.)*

.... 97

Empregada	Pode. Com certeza.
	After you have put it on…
	Que acha?
Você	*(Tell her it doesn't suit you very well.)*
	....
Empregada	Então experimente esta azul.
	You follow her suggestion…
	Esta fica-lhe muito bem, não acha?
Você	*(Say yes, you like this one, it suits you. Ask how much it is.)*
	....
Empregada	São quatro contos e duzentos.
Você	*(Tell her it's not at all expensive — you'll take it.)*
	....

127 Check the full dialogue on your cassette. If you want further practice, write out your side of the dialogue and then check it in the **Key**.

'It's too / very…'

128

26 You have learned how to use **muito** when saying 'Thank you very much' or 'I'm very well'. You can also use **muito** to say 'it's too…'.

Maria is exploring the local fair (**a feira**), hoping to buy a tablecloth (**uma toalha de mesa** — literally 'a table towel'). She picks out one that she likes and asks the price. Listen particularly to how she tells the **vendedora** (the seller, the stall-holder) that it's too expensive.

Maria	Boa tarde. Tem toalhas de mesa?
Vendedora	Tenho sim, minha senhora. Tenho estas toalhas bordadas que são muito bonitas.
Maria	Gosto muito desta. Quanto é?
Vendedora	São cinco contos.
Maria	Ah — é muito cara. É caríssima! Não tem mais baratas?

bordado *embroidered*
bonito *pretty*
barato *cheap*

To say it's very / too…: **É muito…**

É muito { grande / caro / barato   *It's very / too* { *big / dear, expensive / cheap*

You may also hear the ending **-íssimo**. This can be added to many words to emphasise the idea of 'very': **É caríssimo!** 'It's *very* expensive!' See **Grammar 6.6** for further explanation.

Cheaper / more expensive

27 You are already familiar with the word for 'more' — as in **mais alguma coisa?**, for example.

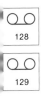

Listen again to the previous dialogue. Notice particularly how Maria asks **a vendedora** if she has any cheaper ones.

Now carry on with your cassette. Maria is still trying to choose. The one she is looking at now is too small (**pequeno**). Listen to how **a vendedora** says 'This one is bigger'.

Maria	Esta é muito pequena.
Vendedora	Faz favor de ver esta aqui. Esta é maior. É muito bonita, não acha?
Maria	Ah sim. Esta é linda, e é maior do que aquela. Quanto é?
Vendedora	São quatro contos.

lindo   *lovely*

To say *'This one is cheaper/more expensive'* etc.:

Este
Esta } é mais { barato/a
caro/a
pequeno/a
bonito/a } This one is {
cheaper
more expensive
smaller
prettier

But you don't use **mais** with **grande**, **bom** or **mau** (bad); to say *'This one is bigger/better/worse'*:

Este
Esta } é { maior
melhor
pior } This one is { bigger
better
worse

To compare things use **do que**:

**Este casaco é maior
do que aquele**   *This jacket is bigger
than that one*

**Aquela blusa é mais bonita
do que esta**   *That blouse is prettier
than this one*

The cheapest/most expensive

28   Maria has still not found a tablecloth to her satisfaction. Listen now to how she asks which are the cheapest.

Maria	Gosto muito desta. Quanto é?
Vendedora	São três contos e novecentos.
Maria	É cara. Quais são as mais baratas?
Vendedora	As mais baratas são aquelas. Também são de boa qualidade, mas são mais pequenas.
Maria	Posso vê-las?

Posso vê-las?   *May I see them?* (**ver** + **as**)

To say *'the most...'*, *'the... -est'*, use **o mais**...
(BUT **o maior**, **o melhor**, **o pior**):

Este café é o mais barato   *This coffee is the cheapest*
Este hotel é o melhor   *This hotel is the best*
Aquelas calças são as maiores   *Those trousers are the biggest*

99

29 Now for some more practice. First of all identify which of the incomplete statements in **30** refers to which picture. In some cases it is obvious, in others less so, so check in the **Key** before you carry on.

30 Now look at the picture that belongs to each statement and complete the statement in an appropriate way with the words for 'is bigger than', 'is worse than' and so on. To help you, a clue to the kind of comparison being made is given in English for each statement.

1. *(Cost)* O presunto é .... o chouriço.
2. *(Size)* A lata de azeite é .... a garrafa de óleo.
3. *(Quality)* O vinho à direita é .... o vinho à esquerda.
4. *(Cost)* O arroz é .... o café.
5. *(Size)* O frasco de mel é .... o pacote de açúcar.
6. *('Goodness')* O homem à esquerda é .... o homem à direita.
7. *(Cost)* A blusa de algodão é .... a blusa de seda.
8. *(Size)* O postal é .... o selo.
9. *(Cost)* O casaco é .... as calças.
10. *(Size)* A saia é .... o vestido.

Now check your answers on the cassette and / or in the **Key.**

31 If you would like some more practice with numbers, write answers to the following questions. Remember that the answer to **Quanto é...?** begins **São...** If you're not sure how to answer the question **A como é...?**, have another look at section 13.

1. A como é o presunto?
2. Quanto é a blusa de seda?
3. Quanto são as calças?
4. A como é o chouriço?

5. A como é o café?
6. A como é o arroz?
7. Quanto é o casaco?

Check your answers in the **Key**.

'I prefer this one'

32 Finally, you may need to say which of various possibilities you prefer.

In the next two dialogues people are shopping in a rural market. Listen particularly to how they say which items they prefer.

Ana is looking for a basket (**um cesto**).

132

Ana	Faz favor. Posso ver aqueles cestos.
Vendedora	Com certeza, minha senhora. São de muito boa qualidade.
Ana	Gosto deste, mas é muito pequeno. Tem outro maior, do mesmo estilo?
Vendedora	Tenho. Veja este... ou este aqui.
Ana	Os dois são lindos.
Vendedora	Qual prefere?
Ana	Acho que prefiro este. Quanto é?
Vendedora	São quinhentos escudos.
Ana	Está bem. Levo este.

do mesmo estilo *in the same style*
Veja este *Have a look at this one*

133

Francisco wants to buy a jug (**um jarro**), but first he has to find the pottery stall. He asks one of the stall-holders.

Francisco	Desculpe. Onde é que posso comprar artigos de louça e cerâmica?
Vendedora	Há um oleiro que vende aqui perto, daquele lado da praça.
Francisco	Obrigado.

Minutos depois...

Francisco	Boa tarde. Tem jarros?
Oleiro	Tenho muitos! Faz favor de ver. Este vermelho é muito bonito, não acha?
Francisco	É. Mas prefiro o amarelo. Quanto é?
Oleiro	São quatrocentos e vinte escudos.
Francisco	Não é nada caro. Está bem. Levo-o.

um artigo *un article*
a louça *crockery*
a cerâmica *ceramics*

um oleiro *a potter*
vermelho *red*
amarelo *yellow*

> Being asked which one you prefer: **Qual prefere?**
>
> To say 'I prefer { this / that } one': **Prefiro { este / aquele**

101

Resumo

To ask 'Is there still some…?': **Ainda há…?**

To say 'There's { no… left': **Já não há…**

{ none left': **Já não há.**

To say 'I/We have to…'   **Tenho/Temos de…**

To say { 'I/We need a…'   **Preciso/Precisamos dum/duma…**

{ 'I/We need to…'   **Preciso/Precisamos de…**

To ask { if you may/can do something: { **Posso…?**

{ **Podemos…?**

{ where you can do something: { **Onde posso…?**

{ **Onde podemos…?**

To ask the price (per kg. etc.):   **A como** { **é…?**

{ **são…?**

To ask 'May I have a look at some…?' **Posso ver um/uma…?**

To ask 'May I try it/them (on)?' **Posso** { **provᇭ** { **lo?**

{ **experimentᇭ** { **la?**

{ **los?**

{ **las?**

To ask 'What do you think?' **Que** }

(i.e. 'What's your opinion?'): **O que** } **acha?**

To say 'I think that…': **Acho que…**

To say { 'It suits me':   **Fica-** { **me** } **bem**

{ 'It suits you':   { **lhe** }

{ 'It doesn't suit me':   **Não** { **me** } **fica bem**

{ 'It doesn't suit you':   { **lhe** }

To say 'It's very/too…': **É muito…**

To say 'This one is { smaller':

{ more expensive':

{ cheaper':

{ etc.

Este/Esta é mais { **pequeno/a**

{ **caro/a**

{ **barato/a**

{ **etc.**

To say 'This one is { bigger':   **Este/Esta é** { **maior**

{ better':   { **melhor**

{ worse':   { **pior**

To say 'This one is more…   **Este/Esta é mais… do que**

(or …er) than that one':   **aquele/aquela**

Being asked which one you prefer: **Qual prefere?**

To say 'I prefer { this one':   **Prefiro** { **este/esta**

{ the cheaper one':   { **o/a mais barato/a**

To say 'I'll take this one': **Levo este/esta**

To say 'I'll take it':   **Levo-** { **o**

{ **a**

102

Vocabulário A complete list of the words for things you might want to buy would be enormous, and even just the items that have cropped up in this unit make the following list longer than usual. Don't necessarily try to learn all of this at one go. You may be more interested in some kinds of words than others — e.g. to do with food rather than clothes, or vice-versa. Remember, it's more useful to practise the skills in the **Resumo** section than to know the word for every item of clothing you might wear or want to buy. You will soon get used to using a dictionary to find the words you need, and to fitting them into the slots. Hotels often have laundry lists with English translations, and although the translations are not always reliable you might find one of these lists useful if you are shopping for clothes.

ir às compras	esperar	o azeite	a cor
comprar	a bicha	o óleo	amarelo
vender	estar com fome	a marmelada	encarnado
alugar	o pão	o doce de	vermelho
abrir	a padaria	laranja	castanho
fechar	o talho	o mel	azul
o dinheiro	a charcutaria	a papelaria	cinzento
um conto	a mercearia	um postal	um artigo
cambiar	a feira	um selo	a louça
trocar	o mercado	o algodão	a cerâmica
o troco	o supermercado	a lã	um cesto
a libra	um grama	a seda	uma toalha
o dólar	um quilo	o casaco	uma toalha
um cartão	um litro	a camisola	de mesa
a chapa	uma dúzia	a blusa	bordado
entregar	um pacote	o vestido	
receber	uma lata	a saia	também
o balcão	um frasco	as calças	bastante
a caixa	uma caixa	os sapatos	
		apertado	

Mais alguma coisa?

While preparing the *Discovering Portuguese* television programmes, we talked in Ponte de Lima in the Minho to Maria do Céu of the local tourist office about the importance of the fortnightly fair, one of the largest and most colourful markets in Portugal. Here is part of her reply, adapted slightly for you to read. If you have difficulty with some of the words, consult the **Glossary**.

É o mercado mais importante da região. Data de 1225, portanto é também o mercado mais antigo do país. No dia da feira todas as pessoas da região e todas as pessoas de Ponte de Lima vêm fazer as suas compras e as suas vendas. É realmente muito importante para a região, e eu acho que vai continuar assim.

São muitas as coisas que se vendem: todos os animais — as vacas, os porcos, as galinhas — todos os produtos agrícolas da região, todos os produtos da terra. As mulheres da região vêm vender as suas coisas, e outros vêm comprar.

Os turistas que nos visitam compram artesanato. Como sabe, é uma região muito rica em artesanato — o linho, os cestos, etc.

*Selling to the tourist —
a street market in Nazaré*

*Plate painting in
Redondo, Alentejo*

O artesanato

One of the delights of travelling in Portugal is to browse in the country
fairs and markets. Portugal has an enormously rich tradition of craft
work: pottery, embroidery, lace, hand-painted furniture (in the
Alentejo), basket-work, work in gold, silver, copper and tin — the list is
endless. You can still find on sale the tools of many traditional trades —
a distaff for spinning wool by hand, a copper still for distilling **bagaço**
(spirit made from the left-overs of wine-making), a brand-new ox-cart of
a design that has hardly changed since Roman times. All of this
provides fascination for the tourist. And yet…

To the extent that these craft products are still an integral part of the
local way of life, they indicate an enormous gap between the culture
and standards of living of rural areas and those of the city. More so
than almost anywhere else in Western Europe, in Portugal the country
market and, say, the boutique in the latest **Centro Comercial** in
Lisbon seem to belong to two different worlds.

This state of affairs is partly a consequence of the long years of Salazar's
regime, which attempted to isolate Portugal from 'contamination' by
the industrial world of the twentieth century, and idealised the peasant
life as supposedly an incarnation of traditional national values. Since
the 1960s, however, as a result of emigration, tourism and other
pressures to modernise the economy, the pace of change in rural
Portugal has quickened. This process will accelerate further, if
Portuguese agriculture is to become competitive in the context of the
EEC. So what will become of the traditional artisans?

104

Some of their more functional products are superior to the factory-produced alternative. For example, the potters in and around Bisalhães, a village just outside Vila Real in Trás-os-Montes, produce a pot for cooking rice which is far more sophisticated than its 'modern' equivalent. The black, unglazed pot, hardened in a primitive oven — a hole dug in the ground — may seem quaintly outdated, but you can leave it in the oven and take out perfectly cooked rice from which the excess liquid has evaporated through the pot. However, the survival of pottery in Bisalhães may depend less on its intrinsic merits than on factors beyond local control — the appeal of emigration, the rivalry of modern products promoted by glossy advertising, even the construction of a motorway from the Spanish frontier to the coast, by-passing the old road from Vila Real to Oporto where the potters used to sell their wares. Once the village had some fifty potters — more or less the entire population; today there are half a dozen.

As the original local demand for traditional craft products declines, alternative markets can be found to some extent — particularly through tourism, both national and foreign. Many artisans, especially those making objects that are mainly decorative, find an outlet for their wares through the tourist trade. But some crafts are unlikely to survive, or will survive only at the cost of making a product that has lost its original function and meaning. When the ox is completely replaced by the tractor, will the intricate Minho ox-yoke still be a yoke if it is made only for the tourist, to be hung on the wall or converted into a bed-head?

Basket making

6 QUEM FALA?

This unit employs the situation of using the phone to introduce language which is useful both when speaking on the telephone and in other situations — for example, asking how something works, taking leave of someone, making an appointment to meet someone.

Unit 6 completes this part of the course and the emphasis here is particularly on revision, especially in the section **Mais alguma coisa?** which provides an opportunity for you to practise much of what you have learned so far.

How does it work?

1   Peter wants to make a phone-call to London, but he is unfamiliar with Portuguese telephones and wants to learn how to use them. Joana offers to go with him to the post office to explain what to do.

Listen particularly to the way Peter asks how it works.

Joana	Boa tarde. Queríamos fazer uma chamada para Inglaterra.
Empregada	Podem ir para a cabine n.º 4.

Momentos depois...

Peter	Então, como funciona? O que tenho de fazer?
Joana	Bem. Primeiro tem de marcar o indicativo internacional, que é 00, e depois o indicativo de Inglaterra.
Peter	Não sei qual é.
Joana	Podemos consultar a lista telefónica... Aqui está. Para Inglaterra o indicativo é 44. Depois marque o indicativo da cidade e depois o número do telefone.
Peter	Está bem. Obrigado.

fazer uma chamada   *to make a call*
a cabine   *the booth*
marcar o indicativo   *to dial the code*
a lista telefónica   *the telephone directory*

But there is something the matter with the phone. Listen to how Peter says he has the impression it isn't working, and to the **empregada's** comment.

Peter	Desculpe. Tenho a impressão que não funciona.
Empregada	Então o telefone deve estar avariado. Vá para a cabine n.º 5. Entretanto eu vou ligar. Qual é o número?
Peter	É Londres, 246 8000.

avariado   *out of order*
entretanto   *meanwhile*
ligar   *to make the connection* (literally *'to link'*)

To ask how something works: **Como funciona?**
To say *'It doesn't work'*:   **Não funciona**

To say *'It* $\left\{\begin{array}{l} \textit{is out of order'}: \\ \textit{has broken down'}: \\ \textit{isn't working'}: \end{array}\right\}$ **Está avariado**

O meu relógio está avariado   *My watch isn't working*
A luz não funciona   *The light isn't working*

---

2   Now try some practice. Here are two problems for you to sort out.

Your car, parked outside your hotel, won't start. As you peer helplessly at the engine, the hotel porter comes out. 'A garage' is **uma garagem.**

Porteiro	Boa tarde. Qual é o problema?
Você	*(Greet him, and say 'It's broken down'.)*

....

Porteiro	Eu posso telefonar para uma garagem…
Você	*(Say 'No, thank you, I'm going to catch the bus'.)*

....

Check your answer on the cassette and / or in the **Key.**

It isn't your day! You go back into the hotel and press the lift button to go up to your room. Nothing happens. You go to the reception desk. (If you want to remind yourself of some of the words needed here, consult **Vocabulário** at the end of Unit 4.)

Você	*(Say 'Excuse me. Isn't the lift working?')*

....

Recepção	Lamento muito. Está avariado.
Você	*(Say 'But my room's on the sixth floor!')*

....

Recepção	Estão a repará-lo agora. Pode esperar um pouco? *(What is she telling you? And asking you?)*
Você	*(Say 'Yes, I can'. Tell her your car has broken down as well.)*

....

Recepção	Está com azar!

Check your answers on the cassette and / or in the **Key.**

107

Good luck!

3   The Portuguese have different words for 'luck', depending on whether it's 'good luck' (**a sorte**) or 'bad luck' (**o azar**). To wish someone 'Good luck' you say **Boa sorte. Estou com azar** means 'I'm having bad luck', or 'It's not my lucky day'.

Answering the phone

4   In order to use the phone you need to know what to say when the receiver is picked up, and how to say who you are, and who you want to speak to.

Jaime is phoning his office, and asking to speak to the Director. Notice what the secretary says when she picks up the receiver.

Secretária	Estou.
Jaime	Posso falar com o director?
Secretária	Quem é que fala?
Jaime	Fala Jaime Rodrigues.
Secretária	Ah, boa tarde, Sr. Doutor. Como está?
Jaime	Estou bem, obrigado. E a Dona Helena?
Secretária	Assim, assim, Sr. Doutor. Só um momento. Vou ligar.
Jaime	Obrigado.

assim, assim   *so so*

Now listen again to the previous dialogue. This time notice particularly how the secretary asks who is speaking, and how Jaime replies.

> To answer the phone, say: { **Estou**   *('I'm here.')*
>   { **Está?**   *('Are you there?')*
>
> To ask who is speaking: **Quem (é que) fala?**
>
> To say *'This is… speaking'*:   **Fala…**

Margarida is phoning a business colleague. Listen particularly to how she says she would like to speak to Sr. Antunes, and how she asks 'When can I speak to him?'.

Secretária	Está?
Margarida	Boa tarde. Queria falar com o Sr. Antunes.
Secretária	Quem fala, por favor?
Margarida	Fala Margarida Branco.
Secretária	Ah, boa tarde, Sra. Doutora. Olhe, neste momento o Sr. Antunes não está.
Margarida	Quando é que posso falar com ele?
Secretária	Olhe, o Sr. Antunes está numa reunião. A Sra. Doutora não quer deixar um recado?
Margarida	Sim. Faz favor de lhe dizer que até às seis horas estou no 78 52 01.
Secretária	Um momento só. Vou apontar… Portanto, 78 52 01. Está bem.
Margarida	Pronto. Obrigada.

uma reunião   *a meeting*
deixar um recado   *to leave a message*
apontar   *to make a note*

> To say *'I'd like to speak to…'*: **Queria falar com…**
>
> **Queria falar com** { o Sr. Antunes / a Sra. Doutora Branco
> ele, ela *('… to him', '… to her')*
>
> **Quer falar comigo?** *Do you want to speak to me?*
>
> For further guidance, see **Grammar 7.3**

142

5   Now try making a phone-call yourself. The situation is as follows.
You are João Gomes, your refrigerator (**o frigorífico**) has broken down,
it is 9.00 a.m. and you are phoning the electrician, Sr. Martins.

When you start your cassette, you will hear the ringing tone, and
Sr. Martins's assistant, **a empregada,** will answer.

Speak your part in the following dialogue.

Empregada	Está?
Você	……………………………………………………………………………
Empregada	Quem é que fala?
Você	……………………………………………………………………………
Empregada	Bom dia, Sr. Gomes. Qual é o problema?
Você	*(Say that your fridge has broken down and that you would like to speak to Sr. Martins.)*
	……………………………………………………………………………
Empregada	O Sr. Martins ainda não está.
Você	*(Ask when you can talk to him.)*
	……………………………………………………………………………
Empregada	Ele deve chegar às 9.30.

143

Check your answers on the cassette and / or in the **Key.**

'I'll… again'

6   In the next two phone conversations, the callers don't manage to speak
to the people they need to contact. Listen particularly to how they say
'I'll phone again shortly/in a week's time'. Don't worry if you don't
understand everything: we'll return to these conversations in a moment.

144

Julião	Bom dia. Fala Julião Silva. Queria falar com o Sr. Engenheiro Macedo.
Secretária	Um momentinho… Desculpe. O telefone dele está impedido.
Julião	Não faz mal. Telefono outra vez daqui a pouco. Até já.

impedido   *engaged*
daqui a pouco   *shortly* (daqui = de + aqui)

145

Rosa	Boa noite, Sr. Tavares. Posso falar com o João?
Sr. Tavares	Olhe, o João está de férias. Quer deixar um recado?
Rosa	Não, obrigada. Quando é que ele volta?
Sr. Tavares	Vem na próxima quarta-feira.
Rosa	Então, volto a telefonar daqui a uma semana.
Sr. Tavares	Até para a semana.
Rosa	Obrigada. Até para a semana.

de férias   *on holiday*
daqui a uma semana   *in a week's time*
Prazer em ouvi-la   *Nice to speak to you* (literally *'A pleasure to hear you'*)   109

> To say 'I'll... again', use **volto a** and add the word for the action
> OR
> Use the word for the action, and add **outra vez**
>
> To say (you'll do something) in... time, use **daqui a...**
>
> **Volto a telefonar** ⎫
> **Telefono outra vez** ⎬ **daqui a** ⎰ **pouco** *(shortly)*
> *(I'll phone again)* ⎭ ⎨ **uns dias** *(in a few days)*
> ⎱ **uma semana** *(in a week)*

Taking leave

7 You learned in the first unit how to take leave of someone by using
the same phrases as you use for greetings: **bom dia, boa tarde** or **boa
noite.** As in English, when taking leave of each other, people often
refer to the next time they'll meet or speak to each other.

Listen again to the previous two dialogues, and then carry on to the
next one. Pay particular attention to how the speakers finish the
conversation.

Luís	Boa tarde. Queria falar com a Inês.
Inês	Sou eu.
Luís	Daqui fala o Luís.
Inês	Olá! Está bom?
Luís	Estou. E você?
Inês	Óptima! Quando é que nos podemos encontrar?
Luís	Dá jeito amanhã?
Inês	Não. Amanhã não me dá muito jeito. Pode ser sexta-feira?
Luís	Está bem. Até sexta, então.
Inês	Adeus. Até sexta.

daqui fala... *this is... speaking*
olá *hello*
dá jeito *is it convenient?*
adeus *goodbye*

> To take leave of someone, use **até** and add the appropriate
> word(s) to indicate when you expect to meet / speak again.
>
> When you will speak to / see the person again
> in a moment, very soon ⎰ **já**
> later the same day ⎸ **logo**
> at a specific time the same day ⎸ **até** ⎨ **às 4.00,** etc.
> on a specific day ⎸ **domingo,** etc.
> next week ⎸ **para a semana**
> some time in the future ⎱ **à próxima**

8 Now you have another phone-call to make. You are still João Gomes,
and your refrigerator is still **avariado.** You call Sr. Martins again at
10.00, as arranged.

Empregada	Estou… Quem fala?
Você	*(Answer and ask if Sr. Martins is there yet.)*
	………………………………………………………………………………
Empregada	Olhe, Sr. Gomes, afinal o Sr. Martins não vem hoje de manhã. Tem de fazer um trabalho urgente noutro sítio.
Você	*(Ask when you can talk to him.)*
	………………………………………………………………………………
Empregada	Hoje à tarde está de certeza, a partir das 2.30.
Você	*(Say 'Fine, I'll phone again this afternoon'.)*
	………………………………………………………………………………
Empregada	Então até logo, Sr. Gomes.
Você	………………………………………………………………………………

noutro sítio   *somewhere else* (literally '*in another place*')
de certeza   *certainly*
a partir das…   *from… onwards*

Check your answers on the cassette and/or in the **Key**.

Making an appointment

9 In an earlier dialogue, Margarida Branco was phoning Sr. Antunes and left the message that she would be at a particular number until 6.00. By 6.00 he has not phoned back, so she tries again. Sr. Antunes is still not available.

Listen out for how she asks if she may make an appointment to meet him.

Secretária	Estou.
Margarida	Boa tarde. Fala Margarida Branco.
Secretária	Ah sim. Como está, Sra. Doutora?
Margarida	Estou bem, obrigada. E a Dona Maria?
Secretária	Muito bem, obrigada.
Margarida	Já está o Sr. Antunes?
Secretária	Lamento muito, mas o Sr. Antunes ainda não está.
Margarida	Então, eu queria marcar um encontro com ele.
Secretária	Está bem, Sra. Doutora. Só um momento… Ele está livre amanhã de manhã. Pode ser às dez horas, por exemplo?
Margarida	Às dez? Sim, está bem. Olhe, eu queria levar um colega também.
Secretária	Com certeza. Então fica combinado. Até amanhã, Sra. Doutora.
Margarida	Até amanhã. Obrigada.

livre   *free*
amanhã de manhã   *tomorrow morning*
fica combinado   *that's all fixed*

Next morning Margarida and her colleague, Sr. Teixeira, go to Sr. Antunes's office shortly before 10.00. In her exchange with the secretary, listen out for how she says they have an appointment with Sr. Antunes.

111

Margarida	Bom dia, Dona Maria.
Secretária	Ah Sra. Doutora! Bom dia, como está?
Margarida	Estou bem, obrigada. O Sr. Antunes está?
Secretária	Não, ainda não está.
Margarida	Mas temos um encontro marcado com ele para as 10.00!
Secretária	Já sei, Sra. Doutora. Não se preocupe. Ele não deve demorar muito. Sentem-se, por favor. Querem tomar um café?
Margarida	Não, obrigada.
Sr. Teixeira	Eu também não, obrigado.

não se preocupe *don't worry*
não deve demorar muito *he shouldn't be very long*

To say you would like to arrange an appointment with…:
Queria marcar um encontro com…

To say *'That's settled / agreed'* (referring to an appointment):
Fica combinado

To say you have an appointment arranged for… o'clock:
Tenho um encontro marcado para as…

Introductions

10 Sr. Antunes is finally available. Listen particularly to how Margarida introduces Sr. Teixeira, and to what he and Sr. Antunes say to each other.

151

Secretária	O Sr. Antunes já está livre. Podem entrar.
Margarida	Obrigada.

They go into his office…

Sr. Antunes	Bom dia. Como está? Há muito tempo que estão à minha espera?
Margarida	Só alguns minutos.
Sr. Antunes	Peço imensa desculpa.
Margarida	Não faz mal. Olhe, queria apresentar o meu colega… Rui Teixeira.
Sr. Antunes	José Antunes… Muito prazer.
Sr. Teixeira	Muito prazer.

à minha espera *waiting for me*
peço imensa desculpa *I'm extremely sorry*

To introduce someone, begin:
Queria apresentar… *I'd like to introduce…*

Queria apresentar	o meu colega a minha colega }	… *my colleague*
	o meu marido	… *my husband*
	a minha mulher	… *my wife*
	o meu amigo a minha amiga }	… *my friend*

When introduced to someone say: **Muito prazer**

Forms of address

11   As you may have noticed, when referring to someone by his/her title, you use **o / a**, e. g. **Queria falar com o Sr. Antunes.** In a more informal situation, you can also use **o / a** with first names, e. g. **Queria falar com o João; Daqui fala a Margarida.**

You may also have noticed some new forms of address in the previous dialogues: **Dona Maria, Sr. Doutor.**

Dona, followed by the first name, is a familiar but respectful form of address when talking to a woman. The masculine word is **Dom,** but this is only used with the name of a king, an aristocrat, or a bishop. Where in English you would say 'King…', in Portuguese you say, for example, **Dom Pedro V, Dom Manuel II.** It is normally abbreviated to **D.,** and you will come across its use in street-names, e. g. **Praça D. Pedro IV, Rua D. Francisco Manuel de Melo.**

Words for professional occupations are often used in Portugal both when referring to people and when addressing them directly, e. g. **Sr. Engenheiro** or **Sr. Arquitecto.** The most widely used is **Sr. Doutor,** which is a formal way of addressing anyone who has a university degree. It doesn't necessarily indicate that the person is a medical doctor, nor that he has a university doctorate of any kind.

These forms of address indicate a traditional respect for learning. They used to indicate also a high degree of class consciousness and an equation of education with social status, since under the Salazar regime access to higher education was restricted to a small social elite. With the much wider availability of university courses since 1974, to address someone as **Senhor Doutor** no longer necessarily implies, as it often did in the past, a relationship of inequality and an attitude of deference.

There is also **Sra. Doutora.** Although in many ways Portuguese society is **'machista',** at least within the professional middle class women more frequently occupy positions of responsibility than, for example, in the UK.

Diminutives

12   In the dialogue in section 6, the secretary used the words **um momentinho** (a little moment). You will frequently come across words ending in **-inho** or **-inha,** and if you take away this ending what you are left with may be a word that you recognise.

The **-inho** ending often indicates smallness: **uma casa** (a house), **uma casinha** (a little house); **um bocado** (a bit), **um bocadinho** (a little bit); **só um momento** (just a moment), **só um momentinho** (just a little moment). However, these 'diminutive' endings are not necessarily a statement about size. They often convey one of a wide range of attitudes, such as familiarity, affection, pity, irony, and even contempt. Here are a few examples.

Coitado!	*Poor thing!*	Coitadinho!	*Poor little thing!*
Adeus	*Goodbye*	Adeusinho	*Bye bye*
Obrigado	*Thank you*	Obrigadinho	*Thanks*

Vamos tomar um café   *Let's have a coffee*
Vamos tomar um cafezinho?   *How about a nice cup of coffee?*

Resumo

To ask how something works: **Como funciona?**
To say 'It doesn't work': **Não funciona**

To say 'It $\begin{cases} \text{is out of order':} \\ \text{has broken down':} \\ \text{isn't working':} \end{cases}$ **Está avariado**

To answer the phone, say: $\begin{cases} \textbf{Estou} \\ \textbf{Está?} \end{cases}$

To ask who is speaking: **Quem (é que) fala?**
To say 'This is… speaking': **Fala…**

To say 'I'd like to speak to…': **Queria falar com…**

To say 'I'll phone again': $\begin{cases} \textbf{Telefono outra vez} \\ \textbf{Volto a telefonar} \end{cases}$

To say 'in $\begin{cases} \text{a few} \\ \text{ten} \end{cases}$ $\begin{cases} \text{minutes':} \\ \text{hours':} \\ \text{days':} \\ \text{weeks':} \end{cases}$ **daqui a** $\begin{cases} \textbf{uns/umas} \\ \textbf{dez} \end{cases}$ $\begin{cases} \textbf{minutos} \\ \textbf{horas} \\ \textbf{dias} \\ \textbf{semanas} \end{cases}$

To say 'See you $\begin{cases} \text{shortly':} \\ \text{later':} \\ \text{at 4.00':} \\ \text{on Saturday':} \\ \text{next week':} \\ \text{some time':} \end{cases}$ **Até** $\begin{cases} \textbf{já} \\ \textbf{logo} \\ \textbf{às 4.00} \\ \textbf{sábado} \\ \textbf{para a semana} \\ \textbf{à próxima} \end{cases}$

To say 'I'd like to make an appointment with…': **Queria marcar um encontro com…**

To say 'I have an appointment for… o'clock': **Tenho um encontro marcado para as…**

To say 'That's agreed/fixed for… o'clock': **Fica combinado para as…**

To introduce someone, begin: **Queria apresentar…**
When introduced to someone, say: **Muito prazer**

Vocabulário

fazer uma chamada
o telefone
a cabine
consultar
a lista telefónica
marcar $\begin{cases} \text{o indicativo} \\ \text{o número} \end{cases}$
ligar
deixar um recado
apontar
olá

prazer em ouvi- $\left.\begin{cases} \text{lo} \\ \text{la} \end{cases}\right.$
estar $\begin{cases} \text{numa reunião} \\ \text{de férias} \end{cases}$
demorar
voltar
entrar
encontrar
um encontro
dá jeito
livre
à $\begin{cases} \text{minha} \\ \text{sua} \end{cases}$ espera

a partir das…
amanhã de manhã
entretanto
pedir desculpa
preocupar-se
a garagem
reparar

Mais alguma coisa?

This part of the unit provides you with a series of linked situations in which you can practise your Portuguese. Treat it as an opportunity to revise, and if you discover you have difficulties refer back to the relevant unit earlier in the book.

In each of the dialogues that follow, one side of the conversation is given on your cassette. Speak your part of the dialogue, and use your pause button if you need to give yourself more time to think.

At regular intervals the cassette will give you a full version of the dialogue you have just been engaged in. Remember, however, that there is often more than one way of saying things. So if what you have said at a particular point differs slightly from the cassette, it is not necessarily incorrect. The Key gives you your part of the dialogue, and the more obvious alternatives. If what you have said differs from the Key, and you are doubtful if your version is correct, see if you can find it in one of the earlier dialogues.

For the purposes of the dialogues that follow, it is assumed that you are a woman. Your name is Maria Fox.

Your situation is as follows: you are staying in a hotel in Lisbon, nearing the end of a business trip. You need to have a final discussion with Sr. Sousa Matos, whom you have met several times already. His phone number is 69 00 58. It is 10.00 a.m. and you are in your hotel room.

152

1   You pick up your phone and the receptionist answers.

Recepção   Estou.
Você   *(Greet her and say you need to make a phone-call.)*

....

Recepção   Qual é o número que deseja?
Você   ....
Recepção   69 00 58, sim senhora. Já está a chamar.
Você   *(Thank her.)*

....

The phone is answered by Sr. Sousa Matos's secretary...

Secretária   Estou.
Você   *(Greet her. Say you'd like to speak to Sr. Sousa Matos.)*

....

Secretária   Lamento, mas o telefone dele está impedido.
Você   *(Say you'll phone again shortly.)*

....

153

Check your part on the cassette and / or in the **Key.**

115

2 You try again ten minutes later.

Secretária   Estou.

Você   (*Say 'May I speak to Sr. Sousa Matos?'*)

....

Secretária   Quem é que fala?

Você   ....

Secretária   Um momento só. Já pode falar. (*You're through.*)

Sr. S. M.   Sra. Fox, como está?

Você   (*Say 'I'm fine thanks, and you?'*)

....

Sr. S. M.   Muito bem, obrigado. Olhe, quando é que nos podemos encontrar?

Você   (*Ask if it can be tomorrow morning.*)

....

Sr. S. M.   Com certeza. Podemos combinar para as onze e um quarto, por exemplo?

Você   (*Say 'that's fine, see you tomorrow then'.*)

....

Sr. S. M.   Prazer em ouvi-la. Bom dia. Com licença.

Check your part on the cassette and / or in the **Key**.

3 Next morning you arrive at Sr. Sousa Matos's office shortly after 11.00.

Secretária   Bom dia. Que deseja?

Você   (*Greet her, say who you are, and that you have an appointment with Sr. Sousa Matos at 11.15.*)

....

Secretária   Olhe, Sra. Doutora, o Sr. Matos está numa reunião. Mas está quase a acabar. Não demora muito. Faz favor de se sentar.

Você   (*Thank her.*)

....

Alguns minutos depois…

Você   (*Ask her where the toilet is.*)

....

Secretária   A senhora vai por aqui, e fica ao fundo do corredor.

Uns minutos depois…

Secretária   O Sr. Sousa Matos já está livre. Faz favor de entrar.

You go into his office…

Sr. S. M.   Há muito tempo que está à minha espera?

Você   (*Say 'Only a few minutes'.*)

....

Sr. S. M.   Peço imensa desculpa.

Você   (*Say it doesn't matter.*)

....

Check your part on the cassette and / or in the **Key**.

4   By shortly after 1.00 you have finished your discussion with Sr. Sousa Matos, and it's time for lunch. You have previously persuaded Sr. Sousa Matos to allow you to invite him to lunch. (In reality, this would be extremely difficult! The Portuguese have a strong sense of hospitality and in this situation would insist on paying.)

Você   *(Say 'Shall we have lunch, then?'. Ask him if there's a restaurant nearby.)*

....

Sr. S. M.   Há vários. 'O Pescador', por exemplo, é bastante bom.
Você   *(Ask him if it's far — can you walk there?)*

....

Sr. S. M.   Fica muito perto.

A few minutes later you and Sr. Sousa Matos are entering **O Pescador.** *A waiter approaches…*

Empregado   É para almoçar?
Você   *(Give the appropriate answer, and ask if he has a table for two.)*

....

Empregado   Querem ficar ali junto à janela?
Você   *(Say 'I prefer this table here'.)*

....

Empregado   Está bem.
Você   *(Ask him what today's special dish is.)*

....

Empregado   É Bacalhau à Gomes de Sá.
Você   *(Ask him for the menu.)*

....

Empregado   Sim senhora.

Check your part on the cassette and / or in the **Key.**

5   A few minutes later, the waiter returns.

Empregado   Que desejam?
Você   *(Ask for today's special dish.)*

....

Sr. S. M.   Para mim a carne de porco à Alentejana.
Empregado   E para beber?
Você   *(Order a bottle of the restaurant's own red wine.)*

....

You finish your meal…

Você   *(Call the waiter.)*

....

Empregado   Desejam mais alguma coisa?
Você   *(Ask for two black coffees and the bill.)*

....

*Sr. Sousa Matos invites you to his house tomorrow evening for a farewell party (**uma festa**) in your honour…*

Você	*(Ask him if you may bring (**levar**) your colleague.)*

....

Sr. S. M.	Com certeza. Estão convidados os dois.
Você	*(Ask him where he lives.)*

....

Sr. S. M.	Moro na Parede. Quer apontar a morada? É Rua Dr. João de Menezes, 85, r/c.-Dto.
Você	*(Ask him at what time the party begins.)*

....

Sr. S. M.	Por volta das nove horas.
Você	*(Say 'Goodbye, then, see you tomorrow'.)*

....

Check your part on the cassette and / or in the **Key**.

Next evening you meet your colleague at your hotel and set off for Parede. It is west of Lisbon, on the way to Cascais, so you need to go by train from **a estação do Cais do Sodré.**

6 You call a taxi.

Você	*(Greet the driver.)*

....

Taxista	Boa tarde. Para onde é que vão?
Você	....
Taxista	Sim senhora.

Um quarto de hora mais tarde…

Você	*(You have arrived at the station. Ask the driver how much it is.)*

....

Taxista	São trezentos e vinte escudos.
Você	*(Ask him if he has change for a thousand escudos.)*

....

Taxista	Tenho. Faz favor. *(He hands you your change.)*
Você	....

You go into the station to buy your tickets…

Você	*(Ask for two return tickets to Parede.)*

....

Funcionário	São trezentos e oitenta escudos.
Você	*(Ask him what time the train leaves.)*

....

Funcionário	O próximo é às 7.30. Faltam dez minutos.
Você	*(Ask him which platform it is.)*

....

Funcionário	É a n.º 5, aqui à sua esquerda.
Você	....
Funcionário	De nada, minha senhora.

Check your part on the cassette and / or in the **Key**.

7 You arrive in Parede and come out of the station, but you need to ask the way to **a Rua Dr. João de Menezes.** You stop a passer-by.

Você (*Say 'Excuse me' and ask your question.*)

....

Transeunte A Rua Dr. João de Menezes? Ora bem… Aí no fim deste largo viram à direita. Depois voltam na segunda à esquerda e vão sempre em frente.

Você (*Ask if it's far.*)

....

Transeunte Não. Fica pertinho. São talvez dez minutos a pé… ou menos.

Você (*Thank him.*)

....

Transeunte De nada. Boa noite.

Some ten minutes later you are ringing the door-bell. Sr. Sousa Matos opens the door…

Sr. S. M. Ah! Sra. Fox, como está? Faz favor de entrar. Este é o seu colega?

Você (*Say 'I'd like to introduce Sr. Brown'.*)

....

Sr. S. M. Muito prazer.

Sr. Brown How do you do?

Sr. S. M. O Sr. Brown não fala português?

Você (*Say 'No, he only speaks English'.*)

....

Sr. S. M. Então vou apresentá-lo à minha mulher, que percebe um pouco de inglês. Entretanto, que desejam tomar? Há vinho, há whisky, há gin-tonic, há vários licores. Não sei se preferem uma bebida sem álcool?

Você (*Say yes, you prefer an orange juice —* **um sumo de laranja.***)

....

Sr. S. M. E para o Sr. Brown?

Você (*After consultation, you discover he would like a whisky with water; ask for it on his behalf.*)

....

Horas depois…

Você (*Ask what time it is.*)

....

Sr. S. M. É meia-noite menos um quarto.

Você (*Say 'We have to return to Lisbon — our flight is at 10.30 in the morning'.*)

....

Sr. S. M. Então… Muito boa viagem. E até à próxima.

Você (*Thank him very much, and say goodbye.*)

....

Check your part on the cassette and / or in the **Key.**

A cultura moderna

The previous units have indicated some of the characteristics and problems of a country adjusting, since 1974, both to the end of an empire that began with the fifteenth-century voyages, and to the end of almost half a century of government by an authoritarian regime. The Salazar regime encouraged nostalgia for the imperial past and, until the 1960s at least, succeeded in isolating Portugal from Europe and from what it regarded as 'contamination' by the modern world.

One of the many areas of life which were impoverished by the experience of Salazarism was Portugal's rich literary tradition. Literature suffered both indirectly, for example through the state's rigid control of education, and directly through its stifling censorship. Censorship of authors operated not by inspecting works before they were published but by seizing them afterwards from the bookshops, causing financial loss to the publisher and encouraging self-censorship on the part of writers. Poetry, which has always been a strong tradition in Portugal, perhaps survived censorship more easily than the novel. Following the 25th of April, many creative artists, after decades of opposition to the previous regime, were involved in political activity rather than writing, and it is only in the past few years that a more innovative spirit is apparent.

The 18th-century Mateus palace, near Vila Real, Trás-os-Montes. Contemporary sculpture by João Cutileiro

Centro de Arte Moderna,
Lisbon

The modern tradition in Portuguese painting has fared better than literature. In this area, as in other aspects of Portuguese cultural life, an influential role has been played by the Calouste Gulbenkian Foundation, created in 1956, which has enabled artists to remain independent of state patronage. The Foundation's recently completed **Centro de Arte Moderna,** in Lisbon, contains a fine collection of paintings by contemporary artists.

The Portuguese have always been cinema-lovers, and — more recently — television enthusiasts. In terms of cinema, with some notable exceptions, Portugal's production is much less interesting than that of Brazil. In television, the main fare outside news and documentary programmes are British and American series, and Brazilian **telenovelas** ('soap-operas'). The **telenovela** is having an influence on the language. You now hear people using Brazilian expressions which a few years ago were unknown in Portugal, for example the greeting **Tudo bem?** (literally 'Everything well?').

At the moment, however, the major 'threat' to the language (in the eyes of some Portuguese) is not so much the **telenovela,** but a proposal to reform the system of spelling, including the use of accents, in order to iron out the small differences between European and Brazilian Portuguese. This plan is still subject to official approval by the governments concerned. Many Portuguese think it makes too many concessions to the Brazilians, and, as this book goes to press, it is doubtful if the proposal will be accepted, at least in its present form. 121

Alfama, Lisbon

Part II

ANTOLOGIA

The intention of this anthology is to help you launch out for yourself, and get used to discovering more Portuguese by looking at newspapers, magazines, advertisements and so on, and by listening to people speaking Portuguese.

The anthology consists of a selection of extracts from interviews which were recorded in Portugal in the course of preparing the BBC's **Discovering Portuguese** television programmes. Each extract is recorded on your cassette and you are given a transcript with some notes on language, and a translation into English.

The extracts have been chosen according to two principles. Firstly, they give you a chance to listen to some Portuguese people talking about aspects of life and culture that are dealt with in the first part of the book. So, as far as possible, the order in which the extracts are presented follows the order in which different themes have arisen in earlier units.

The second principle has to do with language. The extracts have been selected to give you some experience of a variety of speakers from different areas and backgrounds. As with English-speakers, you will find some more difficult to understand than others.

Obviously, in conversation, none of us speaks in punctuated sentences. So in providing transcripts that are readable, it has sometimes been necessary to edit the spoken version slightly, for example by altering word order or making a small omission, in order to produce a comprehensible text. However, the texts still retain the flavour of the spoken language. In a few places, larger omissions are made, and have been indicated (…) in the text. None of these changes alters the sense of what is said.

There are a number of ways in which you might use these materials to develop your Portuguese further, some more demanding than others.

To start with the most demanding, you could try listening to an interview before you read the text or the translation. Brief introductions are given, and these will guide you towards what to expect. In two specific cases, texts 4 and 12, we provide some questions in advance which you might try to answer by listening to the cassette before you read the transcript.

However, you may prefer to have more detailed information before you listen. If so, try working on the transcript, with or without the English translation, and then listen to the recording. Finally, some people find it helpful to listen and follow what is being said, using the transcript simultaneously. Several permutations of these activities are possible, and you can come back to this anthology from time to time and use it in different ways.

The language notes are intended to be used in conjunction with the Grammar, particularly to help you extend your knowledge of different tenses. The notes also draw attention to 'sign-post' expressions, used to connect the various parts of an explanation or argument, or to qualify or give emphasis to what is being said. Finally, although it is assumed that the translations will supply the vocabulary you need, the notes provide a little guidance here too, since the translation gives only the meaning that the word has in a particular context, and in some cases this may be rather specialised.

1   O DIA DE CAMÕES E DAS COMUNIDADES

Portugal's national day, as we mentioned earlier, is the 10th of June, **o Dia de Camões,** as it was known until 1974. Camões is the great Portuguese poet of the sixteenth century, the author of the epic *Os Lusíadas* which is built round the story of Vasco da Gama's voyage to India and Portugal's history leading up to it.

The name of the national day was changed, following the military coup of the 25th of April 1974, to **o Dia de Camões e das Comunidades,** linking the voyagers of the past and the more humble migrant workers of recent decades. On 10 June 1986, we asked the Portuguese President, Mário Soares, to explain why Portugal's national day is associated with Camões. Here is his reply.

President
Mário Soares

Bem, em primeiro lugar porque o Dia de Camões é o dia de Portugal...
dia de Portugal, porque Camões é a suprema glória do nosso povo, e é
um poeta que está ligado à nossa própria identidade nacional. Portugal
é um velho país, com mais de oito séculos de história. Mantém as
mesmas fronteiras territoriais na Europa desde há oito séculos, o que
significa que não tem tido evoluções como outros países europeus,
e o seu próprio território tem sido sempre o mesmo. Tem uma cultura
e uma língua que são próprias, cultura essa que está profundamente
entrosada com a cultura europeia — como é natural, visto que somos
um país europeu — mas que tem a sua singularidade própria. Essa
singularidade faz com que Portugal tivesse sido intermediário da
Europa junto do vasto mundo no século XV e XVI, que foram os
nossos períodos de descoberta. E, justamente, o nosso poeta Camões é
o poeta nacional porque ele exprimiu num poema admirável — que são
Os Lusíadas — o génio do português que descobriu o mundo na gesta
da ida até à Índia.

Language notes

1   All of this passage is an answer to a question that began *Why...?*, so
   naturally the answer uses *because...* **Porque** is used both in questions
   (**Porque...?**; see **Grammar 11.2**) and, as here, to mean *because...*:

   porque $\begin{cases} \text{o Dia de Camões é...} \\ \text{Camões é a suprema glória do nosso povo} \\ \text{ele exprimiu... o génio do português} \end{cases}$

2   **Mantém as mesmas fronteiras desde há oito séculos.** On this use of
   the present tense to say what has been happening since some time in
   the past, see **Grammar 9.5**.

3   You are familiar with the use of **ter**, meaning *to have:*

   tem $\begin{cases} \text{uma cultura e uma língua que são próprias} \\ \text{a sua singularidade própria} \end{cases}$

   Ter is also used with the past participle to form compound past tenses
   (see **Grammar 9.9**), e. g.

   ... não tem tido evoluções como outros países europeus
   ... o seu próprio território tem sido sempre o mesmo

4   **Próprio** can mean *own,* or *the... itself:*

   A própria língua é importante. *The language itself is important.*
   Tem uma cultura própria. *It has its own culture / It has a culture of its
   own.*

5   On the use of **esse / essa / isso** *(that),* see **Grammar 3.1**. A common use
   is to refer back to something just mentioned, where in English *this* is
   normally used:

   ... tem a sua singularidade própria. **Essa singularidade**...

PORTUGAL'S NATIONAL DAY

Well, in the first place because Camões Day is Portugal's day...
Portugal's day, because Camões is the supreme glory of our people, and
is a poet who is linked to our national identity itself. Portugal is an old
country, with a history of more than eight centuries. It has kept the
same land frontiers in Europe for eight centuries, which means that it
has not undergone changes like other European countries, and its actual
territory has always been the same. It has a culture and language of its
own, a culture which is closely related to European culture (as is only
natural, since we are a European country) but which has its own
individuality. This individuality enabled Portugal to act as intermediary
between Europe and the vast world beyond, in the fifteenth and
sixteenth centuries, which were our periods of discovery. And our poet
Camões is the national poet precisely because he expresses in an
admirable poem — *The Lusiads* — the genius of the Portuguese who
discovered the world in the great exploit of the voyage to India.

2 QUEM SÃO OS PORTUGUESES?

In the previous interview, President Soares talks about Portugal's
national identity. We asked the novelist José Saramago if one can talk
about characteristics that are essentially Portuguese. In his reply, he
accepts that there is some truth in the national stereotype of a
nostalgic, contemplative people, but points out that there is another
side to the coin, which is sometimes ignored: a history of violence, too.
He refers to the Inquisition, finally abolished in the early nineteenth
century, and to the thirteen-year war against the independence
movements in the African colonies, which was brought to an end
by the events of April 1974.

Eu receio cair nos lugares comuns: que nós somos saudosistas, que
somos contemplativos, que somos melancólicos, que somos espirituais.
Mas, na verdade, é que somos tudo isso. Mas, também, há o outro lado
dessa medalha, porque fomos cruéis, e talvez sejamos ainda. Fizemos
uma guerra que não se distinguiu pelas boas maneiras — se as guerras
têm boas maneiras! Tivemos aqui a Inquisição que queimou os judeus,
e os que não eram judeus. Portanto, somos tão cruéis como qualquer
outro (...)

Mas, dum modo geral, creio que somos pessoas com quem é fácil viver.
Não somos excessivamente orgulhosos, não somos arrogantes, não
temos qualquer ideia duma superioridade rácica, talvez porque
conhecemos muito bem as outras raças. E isso dá-nos talvez uma certa
serenidade no modo de estar, na vida, e neste mundo que é o único
que temos, claro.

Language notes

1   You are already familiar with the use of **ser** in such phrases as **sou
português, sou inglesa** and so on. The occurrences of **ser** in this text
provide further examples of how it is used to characterise someone or   127

something, or to define their intrinsic nature. The speaker is characterising the Portuguese:

(não) somos
{
saudosistas
contemplativos
melancólicos
espirituais
cruéis
orgulhosos
arrogantes
}

In contrast, **estar** is used with an adjective when describing a state of affairs, rather than defining the nature of the person or thing, e. g. **Estou bem; estamos cansados; está doente** *(ill)*.

You will find further guidance on **ser** and **estar** in the notes following text 3.

2 On **com quem** *(with whom)*, see **Grammar 8**.

3 The preterite forms of several verbs occur in this text: **fizemos (fazer), distinguiu (distinguir), tivemos (ter)** and **queimou (queimar)**. More will be said about the use of the preterite in the language notes on text 7.

WHO ARE THE PORTUGUESE?

I'm afraid of falling into commonplaces: that we're nostalgic, that we're contemplative, that we're melancholy, that we're spiritual. Though indeed we are all of this. But there is also the other side of the coin, because we have been cruel, and perhaps still are. We made a war that didn't stand out for its good manners — if wars can be good-mannered! We had the Inquisition that burned the Jews, and those that weren't Jews. So we are as cruel as anyone else (...)

But, generally speaking, I think we are people with whom it's easy to live. We're not excessively proud, we're not arrogant, we have no ideas of racial superiority, perhaps because we are very well acquainted with other races. And this perhaps gives us a certain serenity in our way of being, in life, and in this world which is the only one we have, of course.

3 BACALHAU NA CATAPLANA

And now for a more tangible reminder of the importance of the sea in Portuguese culture: Chefe Silva's recipe for **Bacalhau na Cataplana**. The **cataplana** is a pan consisting of two equal halves, hinged together, and locked shut by a metal clip. Its advantage is that it can be turned over from time to time, to give equal heat on both 'top' and 'bottom'. Even without one of these lovely copper pans, you can still try the recipe. Chefe Silva assures us it will work in an ordinary pan.

Remember that you are starting from dried cod, so it has to be soaked for a period that will vary according to the thickness of the pieces. Where no specific quantities are given, Chefe Silva's instruction is **quanto baste** (literally *as much as is enough,* i. e. *according to taste*).

Chef Silva with ingredients for bacalhau na cataplana

Bacalhau na cataplana

4 postas de bacalhau demolhado	4 pieces of soaked cod
1 cebola grande	1 large onion
1 tomate maduro grande	1 large ripe tomato
200 g de presunto	200 g cured ham (Parma-type)
orégãos secos	dried oregano
coentros frescos	fresh coriander
salsa fresca	fresh parsley
meio quilo de gambas	1/2 kg prawns
meio quilo de amêijoas	1/2 kg cockles
1 dl de azeite mal medido	100 ml olive oil, or just under
2 dentes de alho	2 cloves garlic
1,5 dl de vinho branco seco	150 ml dry white wine
1 pimento pequeno	1 small sweet pepper
piri-piri	chilli sauce
sal	salt

Pré-preparação

Demolhe o bacalhau atempadamente. As amêijoas são lavadas e metidas em água com sal (50 g por litro) durante duas horas para perderem a areia.

Descasque e corte a cebola às rodelas, e refogue-a ligeiramente no azeite com os alhos picados e um pouco de pimento. Corte o tomate às rodelas. Corte o restante pimento às rodelas. Pique grosseiramente a salsa e os coentros. Corte o presunto em tiras. Retire as cabeças das gambas.

Preparação

Deite metade da cebola na cataplana e coloque todos os outros elementos às camadas, sem sobrepor o bacalhau, terminando com o resto da cebola, as rodelas de pimento, a salsa, os coentros picados e o vinho branco.

Coloque sobre lume médio durante 15 minutos.

Sirva com cuidado, e abra só na presença de todos, para apreciarem o aroma exalado ao abrir.

129

Language notes

1   Like most recipes, this one illustrates a form of the verb used in instructions (see Unit 4, section 15 and **Grammar 9.11**). The infinitive forms of these particular verbs are:

demolhar	retirar
descascar	deitar (often *to pour;* **deitar-se,** *to lie down*)
cortar	colocar
refogar	servir (**sirvo,** *I serve*)
picar	abrir

You will notice a change of spelling in **descascar (descasque), refogar (refogue), picar (pique)** and **colocar (coloque)**. The **qu,** and the **u** after **g,** are necessary before the vowel **e,** in order to convey the 'hard' consonant sounds (i. e. **c** as in *cat* and **g** as in *got*). Without these spelling changes, the **c** and **g** would be 'softened' by the **e** (i.e. the **c** would sound like the **s** in *some,* and the **g** like the **s** in *measure*).

2   **Ser** is used with the past participle as one way of forming passive constructions in Portuguese (see **Grammar 9.8**):

São $\left\{ \begin{array}{l} \textbf{lavadas} \\ \textbf{metidas em água} \end{array} \right.$ *They are* $\left\{ \begin{array}{l} \textit{washed} \\ \textit{put in water} \end{array} \right.$

Estar is used with the past participle when the latter functions as an adjective, i. e.:

São lavadas *They are washed* (= you wash them)
Estão lavadas *They are washed* (= *they have been washed, they are clean*)

You will find examples of this use of **estar** in several of these texts, e.g. **está ligado** *(it's linked),* **está relacionado** *(it's related).* Text 9 contains examples of both **ser** and **estar** with the past participle, and illustrates the difference.

3   In Portuguese there is a 'personal' infinitive. That is, in certain circumstances endings are added to the infinitive to indicate the subject of the verb. See **Grammar 9.13** and **9.14.** It is very commonly used, and will crop up again in some of the texts that follow.

... **para perderem a areia** *... in order for them to lose the sand*
... **para apreciarem o aroma** *...in order for them to appreciate the aroma.*

CATAPLANA CODFISH

Advance preparation

Soak the dried cod as long as necessary. The cockles are washed and put in salted water (50 g per litre) for two hours to get rid of the sand.

Peel and slice the onion, and fry it gently in the olive oil with the chopped garlic and a little pepper. Slice the tomato. Slice the rest of the pepper into rings. Roughly chop the parsley and coriander. Cut the ham into strips. Remove the heads from the prawns.

Preparation

Put half the onion in the **cataplana** and place the other ingredients in layers, without letting the pieces of cod overlap, finishing with the rest of the onion, the slices of pepper, the parsley, the chopped coriander and the white wine.

Set on a medium flame for 15 minutes.

Serve carefully, and open it with everyone present so that they can appreciate the aroma given off when you open it.

4   A EMIGRAÇÃO (I)

In part of our interview with President Soares on **o Dia de Camões e das Comunidades,** we asked him about the importance of emigration for the Portuguese. His reply suggests that there is a continuity between the voyagers of the fifteenth and sixteenth centuries and the emigrants of more recent times.

If you would like more practice in understanding spoken Portuguese, listen to the cassette before you read the text and see how much of the following information you can extract. Then check your answers in the Portuguese text, using the translation where necessary.

Dr. Soares says that the Portuguese communities abroad are concentrated in certain countries. Which countries does he mention?

What is the approximate total number of Portuguese living abroad? (Two figures are mentioned.)

Dr. Soares goes on to talk about the kinds of links which the emigrants maintain with Portugal. Try to identify some of these links.

Bem, os portugueses foram sempre um povo de emigrantes, porque duma maneira geral nascem suficientes portugueses para se sentirem um pouco comprimidos neste território, que é pequeno, e se lançarem na aventura do desconhecido e na descoberta do mundo. Nós hoje temos comunidades espalhadas um pouco por toda a parte, mas fundamentalmente concentradas nos Estados Unidos, no Brasil, na Austrália, no Canadá, na Europa (particularmente na Europa do Mercado Comum — em França, também em Espanha, em Itália, na Alemanha Federal), e ainda na África do Sul. Isso significa no total cerca de três milhões e meio a quatro milhões de portugueses que vivem dispersos pelo mundo... mas com a peculiaridade de todos se sentirem muito ligados a Portugal, de continuarem a conservar os nossos costumes, a nossa cultura, a nossa língua, a ensinar os seus filhos na língua portuguesa; e, por outro lado, ligados às suas próprias terras, recebendo a imprensa regional dos sítios donde provêm, e tendo uma ligação muito directa com o nosso país que nunca se perde. E isso faz com que esses emigrantes sejam uma força: em primeiro lugar, uma força económica, porque eles enviam muitas das suas economias para as famílias e para Portugal, o que é importante, e, por outro lado, mantêm também um espírito duma grande ligação a Portugal, trazendo as inovações do que aprendem lá fora; mas, por outro lado, levando também os hábitos, os costumes, a nossa literatura, a nossa arte para os países onde trabalham.

131

Language notes

1　There are some further examples of the personal infinitive in this text:

**nascem suficientes portugueses para se sentirem… e se lançarem…
… com a peculiaridade de todos se sentirem… de continuarem…**

In all these cases the **-em** ending helps to make it clear that it is 'they' who are feeling, launching out, etc.

2　There are a number of common phrases here for connecting different parts of an explanation, giving them the emphasis you want, or making a contrast:

duma maneira geral　*generally speaking* (literally *in a general way*)
mas　*but*
ainda　*even* (also, in other contexts, *still*)
isso significa　*this means*
por outro lado　*on the other hand, also* (literally *on the other side*)
em primeiro lugar　*in the first place, firstly*

Por outro lado is often used as one of a pair of phrases introducing a contrast: **por um lado**… *(on the one hand…),* **por outro lado**… *(on the other hand…).*

3　Most words ending **-ndo** in Portuguese are gerunds, and correspond to words ending *-ing* in English: **recebendo** *(receiving),* **tendo** *(having),* **trazendo** *(bringing).*

EMIGRATION (I)

Well, the Portuguese have always been an emigrant people, because generally speaking enough Portuguese are born for them to feel a little constricted in this country, which is small, and for them to venture out into the unknown to discover the world. Today we have communities scattered almost everywhere, but mainly concentrated in the United States, Brazil, Australia, Canada, Europe (particularly the Europe of the Common Market — France, Spain too, Italy, West Germany), and even in South Africa. This means, in all, some three and a half to four million Portuguese who are scattered throughout the world… but distinguished by the fact that they all feel very closely linked to Portugal, that they go on keeping our customs, our culture, our language, and teaching their children in Portuguese; and, also, linked to their own homes, receiving the regional newspapers from the places they come from, and having a very direct link with our country, which they never lose. And this makes these emigrants a force to be reckoned with: first of all, an economic force, because they send much of their savings to their families and to Portugal, which is important, and, on the other hand, because they also maintain a spirit of close relationship with Portugal, bringing back innovations from what they learn outside; but, at the same time, taking with them their habits and customs, our literature, our art to the countries where they work.

5   A EMIGRAÇÃO (II)

In the previous interview, President Soares mentions the long history of emigration and explains the broad context of the present situation. We put some more specific questions to António Manuel Pires Cabral, a teacher and writer from Trás-os-Montes. Here he talks about the economic causes of emigration, the Portuguese attachment to **a terra,** the effects of emigration on family life, and the impact on the local community when the emigrants return.

Q: *Porque é que há tanta emigração?*

A: Em Trás-os-Montes? Porque, naturalmente, somos uma das zonas mais deprimidas economicamente do país. Aliás, todo o Portugal é uma das zonas mais deprimidas da Europa. Para começar, Portugal está na cauda de tudo, e por esse mesmo motivo as pessoas não encontram aqui, enfim, a sua subsistência, de modo que têm mesmo que emigrar.

Q: *Porque é que a maioria dos emigrantes voltam sempre?*

A: Eu penso que isso faz parte da psíquica do povo português. O povo português é uma criatura extraordinariamente apegada à sua própria pátria, à sua terra. De forma que, em princípio, quando vai embora vai sempre levando na bagagem a intenção de voltar.

Q: *E que efeito é que a emigração tem sobre as crianças e sobre a estrutura familiar?*

A: Bom, pode ter algum efeito, porque se é verdade que os pais, normalmente, desejam de facto voltar a Portugal, os seus filhos — portanto, digamos, emigrantes da segunda geração — esses às vezes já é mais difícil convencê-los a voltar. E então pode de facto a emigração ser o elemento disruptor da família.

Q: *E como é que os emigrantes se comportam quando voltam?*

A: Bom, eles são um pouco ruidosos, um pouco insolentes, talvez. Pensam que por terem conquistado a prosperidade, que são realmente reis do país. Mas nós temos que desculpar isso, porque de facto temos que considerar que eles são pessoas que saíram daqui num estado de pobreza total, e justamente saíram porque eram pobres, e que depois de muito trabalho conseguiram de facto conquistar a prosperidade e a riqueza. E então eles querem é mostrá-la, segundo os padrões europeus que se habituaram a admirar lá fora. Simplesmente, eles não têm mecanismos de filtragem suficientes, e portanto quando cá chegam trazem uma série de sinais que, para nós que cá vivemos, acabam por ser um pouco chocantes. É o caso das casas que eles fazem, que não têm nada a ver com as casas da região, que descaracterizam profundamente as nossas aldeias. E é também o caso da linguagem, que trazem na sua bagagem: já não é bem o português; também não é ainda o francês. É aquilo que nós às vezes brincamos — o *françuguês.*

Language notes

1   You are familiar with **ter de**... (e.g. **tenho de ir às compras**);
    ter que... is an alternative way of saying *to have to:*

$$\textbf{têm / temos que} \left\{ \begin{array}{l} \textbf{emigrar} \\ \textbf{desculpar isso} \\ \textbf{considerar que}\ldots \end{array} \right.$$

2   You are also familiar with the question **Ainda há...?** and the answer
    Já não há. There is a similar structure, using **ser,** near the end of this
    text, which shows how versatile this pair of expressions is:

    já não é bem o português   *it's no longer quite Portuguese*
    não é ainda o francês   *it isn't yet French*

3   **Mesmo** often means *same.* It is also used to give emphasis, e.g. **agora
    mesmo** *(right now);* **têm mesmo que emigrar** *(they really have to
    emigrate).*

4   The expression **lá fora** (literally *out there,* i.e. *abroad)* also cropped up
    towards the end of text 4. This phrase itself — the fact that *abroad* is
    thought of as *out there* — suggests the Portuguese attachment to home,
    to **a terra.** It's as though other countries are a large unknown terrain to
    which you go out **na aventura do desconhecido** (text 4), but always
    with the intention of returning.

5   The word **povo** *(people),* which occurs in several of these texts, has no
    single equivalent in modern English. It sometimes means the nation as
    a whole; it often means *the ordinary people.* These two concepts are
    closely linked in Portuguese.

6   Other vocabulary

    Some more phrases which act as links between different parts of an
    explanation, or which qualify or emphasise what you say, are:

    aliás   *besides*   **talvez**   *perhaps*
    de modo que } *so that*   **de facto**   *indeed*
    de forma que }

    You are familiar with **aqui** and **ali** as words for *here* and *there.* **Cá** and **lá**
    also mean *here* and *there.* They normally come before the other word
    they are associated with — the opposite of English word order.

    quando cá chegam   *when they arrive here*
    para nós que cá vivemos   *for us who live here*
    lá fora   *out there*

    Ir(-se) embora is *to go away.* However, you will frequently come across
    embora separate from this expression, usually meaning *although.*

    Brincar means *to play, to joke.*

EMIGRATION (II)

Q: *Why is there so much emigration?*

A: In Trás-os-Montes? Because we are of course one of the most economically depressed areas in the country. Besides, the whole of Portugal is one of the most economically depressed areas in Europe. To begin with, Portugal is at the tail-end of everything, and for that very reason people can't find a livelihood here, so that they just have to emigrate.

Q: *Why is it that the majority of emigrants always come back?*

A: I think that this is part of the mentality of the Portuguese people. The Portuguese are creatures extraordinarily attached to their own country, to their birth-place. So that, in principle, when they go away they always go taking with them the intention to return.

Q: *And what effect does emigration have on the children and on the structure of the family?*

A: Well, it can have some effect, because if it's true that the parents, normally, want in fact to come back to Portugal, their children — that is, let's say, second generation emigrants — they the children, it's more difficult to convince them to return. And therefore emigration can indeed be the disruptive element in the family.

Q: *And how do the emigrants behave when they come back?*

A: Well, they're a bit loud, a bit insolent, perhaps. They think that by having gained prosperity they are really the kings of the country. But we have to forgive that, because in fact we have to consider that they are people who left here in a state of total poverty, and left precisely because they were poor, and that after a lot of work they have managed in fact to gain prosperity and wealth. And so what they want is to show it, according to the European patterns that they have got used to admiring outside. It's simply that they don't have adequate filter mechanisms, and so when they arrive here they bring with them a whole set of signals which, for us living here, become slightly offensive. That's the case with the houses they build, which have nothing to do with the houses of the area and which completely spoil the character of our villages. It's also the case with the language they bring with them: it's no longer really Portuguese; nor is it quite French either. It's what we sometimes call, jokingly — *Frenchuguese.*

Bearing in mind the striking differences between, say, the Minho or Trás-os-Montes on the one hand and, on the other, the Alentejo or the Algarve, we asked the ethnographer Dr. Veiga de Oliveira if there is perhaps more than one Portugal.

In his reply, he refers to a book by the geographer Orlando Ribeiro that has become a classic, *Portugal: o Mediterrâneo e o Atlântico*, which sees Portugal as an amalgamation of northern and Mediterranean climates and cultures.

Dr. Veiga de Oliveira stresses the contrasts between North and South, and the historical origins of these differences: the stronger Roman and Arab influences in the South, and the Germanic influences in the North. He uses two examples to illustrate these differences: the regional style of houses, and the types of plough traditionally used in the areas he refers to.

Verdadeiramente, há só um Portugal. Mas essa unidade, como eu disse, encerra uma grande diversidade. Para começar, há uma diversidade muito marcada entre o Norte e o Sul. Eu insisto: não se pode dizer talvez dois Portugais, mas que há uma diversidade muito grande, isso é um dado de experiência imediata (...)

Para responder mais concisamente, com uma certa base científica e experimental, eu socorrer-me-ei do livro do Orlando Ribeiro, do *Portugal: o Mediterrâneo e o Atlântico*. Quer dizer, o Portugal do Sul, que é de grande influência mediterrânea: é o Portugal que sofreu o maior impacto dos romanos e dos árabes seguidamente. O resto do país, também, evidentemente que esteve sob o domínio dos árabes, mas com influências muito menos profundas. E no Norte, pelo contrário, as influências germânicas. Temos que pensar que Braga foi a capital do reino dos suevos e dos visigodos seguidamente. Quer dizer, há uma diferenciação muito grande que se apoia também em dados históricos (...)

Há no Norte ainda uma divisão da parte ocidental, noroeste digamos (das províncias sobretudo do Minho e Douro Litoral, que vem até ao Douro, mais ou menos) e a parte transmontana, que é a parte mais arcaizante do país, que se diferencia muito nitidamente também do próprio noroeste, separados pela barreira de montanhas que fazem na verdade um esquema muito nítido.

Isto tudo se traduz pelo ponto de vista da cultura, e portanto da identidade nacional de uma maneira muito marcada. O Sul mediterrâneo com as suas aldeias brancas de casas térreas; o Norte com as suas casas de pedras de dois andares: em baixo os animais, em cima a habitação das pessoas, etc. Quer dizer, uma série de dados que marcam muito bem esses contrastes.

E, acima de tudo, eu chamaria a atenção para, por exemplo, o arado, que é uma peça fundamental das culturas rurais, e que está representada em Portugal pelos três tipos que acentuam perfeitamente essas diferenças. No Sul, o arado dos povos mediterrâneos — o arado romano, propriamente dito. No noroeste, o arado germânico, ligado ao milho desde o século XVI, mas enfim antes disto também ligado às terras mais frescas. Do leste, o arado radial, o arado que Jorge Dias considerou até como sendo o arado anterior, o arado lusitânico, que se conservou pelas terras secas — culturas mais arcaicas.

Language notes

1 This text is a complex explanation, carefully structured to make certain broad contrasts (e. g. north / south, east / west) and to elaborate and qualify these contrasts. So it contains many expressions for introducing new stages in the explanation, for stressing certain points, for making contrasts and introducing examples, e. g.

para começar   *to begin with*
para responder mais concisamente   *to answer more concisely*
quer dizer   *that is* (literally *it means*)
evidentemente   *evidently, obviously*
pelo contrário   *on the contrary*
acima de tudo   *above all*
propriamente dito   *properly speaking*
por exemplo   *for example*

2 The notes following text 3 refer to one way of forming the passive in Portuguese, using **ser** and the past participle. Another way, which is more common, is to use the reflexive pronoun **se** with the verb:

não se pode dizer que…   *it can't be said that…*
tudo isto se traduz   *all this is translated*
que se diferencia   *which is differentiated*
que se conservou   *which was preserved*

3 In Portuguese, object pronouns sometimes come before and sometimes follow the verb. This is explained more fully in **Grammar 7.5**. With the future tense, however, in a situation where the pronoun would normally follow the verb, it comes between the main part of the verb and the ending, e. g.

socorrer-se   *to resort to, have recourse to*
socorrer-me-ei   *I'll resort to*

This use of the future tense with pronouns is relatively rare in speech, but crops up in written language. (Often you can 'avoid' the future tense by using the present instead — see **Grammar 9.5**.)

4 This text also contains some more instances of the preterite: **disse** (**dizer**), **foi** (**ser**), **sofreu** (**sofrer**), **esteve** (**estar**). Further explanation is given after text 7.

IS THERE ONLY ONE PORTUGAL?

Really, there is only one Portugal. But this unity, as I have said, contains a great diversity. To start with, there is a very pronounced difference between North and South. I must stress that one can't perhaps say there are two Portugals; but that there is a very great diversity... that is a fact that we recognise immediately (...)

To give you a more concise answer, with some scientific, experimental basis, I'll resort to Orlando Ribeiro's book, *Portugal: the Mediterranean and the Atlantic*. That is, southern Portugal, which has an enormous Mediterranean influence and is the Portugal that underwent the greatest impact from the Romans and then the Arabs. The rest of the country, too, obviously was under Arab domination, but with much less profound influences. And in the North, on the contrary, Germanic influences. We must remember that Braga was the capital of the Suevian kingdom, and then of the Visigoths. In other words, there is a very big distinction, which is also supported by historical data.

In the North there is yet another division: between the western part, let's say the north-west (the provinces particularly of the Minho and coastal Douro, down to the Douro more or less), and the Trás-os-Montes region, which is the most primitive part of the country, and which is also clearly differentiated from the north-west itself, separated as they are by the barrier of mountains, which form a very clear division.

All of this is reflected from the point of view of culture, and therefore of national identity, in a very distinctive way. The Mediterranean South, with its white villages of one-storey houses; the North with its two-storey stone houses: down below, the animals, up above the human dwelling, etc. In other words, there's a whole series of details which underline these contrasts very clearly.

And, above all, I'd draw attention, for example, to the plough, which is a basic part of rural culture, and which in Portugal has three characteristic forms which emphasise these differences perfectly. In the South, the plough of Mediterranean people — or strictly speaking, the Roman plough. In the North-West, the Germanic plough, associated with maize since the sixteenth century, but actually before that also associated with cooler areas. In the East, the 'radial' plough, the plough that Jorge Dias considered perhaps the original plough, the Lusitanian plough, which survived in drier areas — in more primitive cultures.

7 O ALENTEJO E O 25 DE ABRIL (I)

One of the contrasts between North and South, as we mentioned in Unit 4, is the system of land tenure: small-holdings in the North, large estates in the Alentejo. The question of land distribution in the Alentejo, and the occupation of many of the estates by workers in the aftermath of the revolution of the 25th of April 1974, is still a bitterly divisive issue. Here are two very different views of these events, from an agricultural worker and, in text 8, from a landowner.

Q: *Podia-me dizer o significado do 25 de Abril para si, falando um bocadinho da situação antes e depois?*

A: Em relação ao 25 de Abril... Para mim teve um significado bastante importante não só para mim, mas principalmente para os trabalhadores agrícolas. Os trabalhadores agrícolas antes do 25 de Abril tinham uma vida muito mais dura, com bastante mais dificuldade. Viviam só daquilo que lhes queriam dar, com as dificuldades... Foi uma coisa muito difícil viver-se antes do 25 de Abril.

Com o 25 de Abril tudo se modificou. Deixámos de ser explorados pelos patrões, ou seja, pelos antigos agrários que apenas se serviam dos trabalhadores... sei lá... para lhes sugar o suor. E após o 25 de Abril isso não aconteceu.

Teve um significado muito importante, e trouxe bastantes regalias sociais. Por exemplo, o fim de semana — que não tínhamos; como por exemplo férias, que não tínhamos direito a férias antes do 25 de Abril. Portanto fomos os trabalhadores mais explorados do tempo do fascismo, ou seja, antes do 25 de Abril.

Q: *E qual era a situação quando vocês ocuparam as terras?*

A: A situação de nós na altura em que ocupámos as terras... Vivia-se nesta terra — nesta aldeia em que estamos, a aldeia do Freixo — vivia-se aqui sob o desemprego. Nesta altura, no período de Maio até Outubro, as pessoas viviam com a emigração temporária: saíam para o Ribatejo, para a apanha do tomate, para a apanha da uva. Enfim, vivia-se mal, vivia-se aqui mal.

Language notes

1 Talking about the past

The two basic tenses you need in order to talk about past experiences are the preterite and the imperfect. The forms of these tenses for regular verbs and for a selection of the most common irregular verbs are given in **Grammar 9.2** and **9.3**. Their uses are described in **Grammar 9.6** and **9.7**.

You are already familiar with one special use of the imperfect, which in fact has nothing to do with past experience:

Queria... *I'd like...*
Podia...? *Could you...?*

This use crops up in the first question in the above text:

Podia-me dizer…? *Could you tell me?*

In the rest of this note we are concerned with the more common use of the imperfect, as one of the two main tenses needed to talk about the past. English-speakers often have difficulty knowing which of these tenses to use. It's easiest to explain by beginning with the preterite.

The preterite is used to say what someone did, or what happened at some time in the past. It is irrelevant how long the action took to complete: it may be something which happened in a moment, or which lasted for centuries. But when you use the preterite, you are summing it up as a single experience:

Fizemos uma guerra que não se distinguiu pelas boas maneiras (text 2)
Tivemos aqui a Inquisição que queimou os judeus (text 2)
Fomos os trabalhadores mais explorados do tempo do fascismo

The imperfect is used to talk about a situation which was the background to an event or sequence of events, or which was the state of affairs before the event(s) occurred:

Tivemos aqui a Inquisição que queimou os judeus e os que não eram judeus (text 2)
Saíram porque eram pobres (text 5)
Qual era a situação quando vocês ocuparam as terras?

The reply to this last question, in the text above, describes the situation that existed before the occurrence of the event (**ocupámos as terras**), so the imperfect is used throughout the paragraph:

vivia-se sob o desemprego
as pessoas viviam com a emigração
saíam para o Ribatejo
vivia-se mal

Often the preterite is preceded by a word or phrase which indicates the specific moment when the event in question occurred:

Com o 25 de Abril tudo se modificou. Deixámos de ser explorados…
Após o 25 de Abril isso não aconteceu
Qual era a situação quando vocês ocuparam as terras?

2 There are further examples in this text of the passive consisting of **se** combined with the verb. Here, as in the case of **não se pode dizer** (text 6, note 2), the structure is used in an impersonal way, which usually corresponds to the English *one/you/we…*:

vivia-se mal *one/we lived badly*

3 **Sei lá.** This is a colloquial expression meaning *I don't know,* and often used emphatically to mean something like *I haven't the faintest idea.* In other contexts, **sei** is *I know.*

140

Q: *Could you tell me the significance of the 25th of April for you, saying a little bit about the situation before and after?*

A: In relation to the 25th of April… For me it had quite an important significance — not only for me, but mainly for agricultural workers. Agricultural workers before the 25th of April had a much harder life, with a lot more difficulties. They lived just on what people were willing to give them, with difficulty… Life was very difficult before the 25th of April.

With the 25th of April everything changed. We stopped being exploited by the owners, that is, by the previous farmers who simply used the workers… I don't know… to squeeze the last drop of sweat out of them. And after the 25th of April that didn't happen.

It had a very important significance, and it brought quite a lot of social benefits. For example, weekends off — which we didn't have before; like for example holidays, for we didn't have any right to holidays before the 25th of April. So we were the most exploited workers in the fascist period, that is, before the 25th of April.

Q: *And what was the situation when you occupied the land?*

A: Our situation at the time we occupied the land… You lived in this place — in this village where we are, the village of Freixo — you lived here with unemployment. At this time (of year), in the period from May to October, people lived on temporary migration: they would go off to the Ribatejo, for the tomato-picking and grape-picking. So, life was hard, life here was hard.

8 O ALENTEJO E O 25 DE ABRIL (II)

Here is the landowner's account of how his land was occupied.

Q: *Ocuparam-lhe terras também?*

A: Tudo o que era do meu pai foi tudo ocupado. Em Julho de 75, Setembro de 75, Outubro de 75, tudo o que ele tinha foi tudo ocupado. Ficou lá alguma coisa por ocupar, que eram propriedades que eram minhas que tinham sido compradas — adquiridas — há pouco tempo, e onde não havia tanta riqueza como havia nas outras. As do meu pai que tinham bastantes gados, bastantes produtos em armazém, boas alfaias e tractores, pois essas é que foram as ocupadas. O processo foi mesmo de ocupar aquilo que estava explorado, e não o que estava abandonado — ao contrário do que dizia a classe política da altura, o próprio MFA, o Movimento das Forças Armadas, porque estavam em conjunto.

Q: *O que é que fez quando lhe ocuparam as terras?*

A: Praticamente não fiz nada. Não lutei. Não lutei fisicamente, porque era impossível lutar. Era impossível na altura lutar porque as forças militares estavam na ocupação das terras, com os carros de militares, com G-3, com espingardas, acompanhando os trabalhadores na ocupação das herdades. Essa foi a realidade do Alentejo. Quando se diz que foi o trabalhador que foi ocupando, não foi o trabalhador. O trabalhador foi incitado a ocupar pelas forças políticas civis e pelos militares da esquerda.

Language notes

1 This text, too, contains plenty of examples of the use of the preterite and the imperfect. If you want to have a closer look at how these tenses are used here, you may find it helpful to bear in mind particularly the distinction between 'event' (preterite) and 'situation' (imperfect).

2 You use the imperfect of **ter** with the past participle to form the pluperfect, e.g.

tinha comprado   *I had bought*
tínhamos adquirido   *we had acquired*

The examples in this text are of its passive use:

tinham sido $\left\{ \begin{array}{l} \textbf{compradas} \\ \textbf{adquiridas} \end{array} \right.$ *they had been* $\left\{ \begin{array}{l} \textit{bought} \\ \textit{acquired} \end{array} \right.$

3 Vocabulary

Uma alfaia *(an implement).* Words beginning **al-** in Portuguese are often of Arab origin. You will come across them frequently in place-names (e.g. **Algarve** — *'the West').* Another particular area in which they occur commonly is that of vocabulary relating to agriculture and plants. An example you are likely to encounter is **uma alface** *(a lettuce).*

A classe política. The word **classe** is used here not in the sense of *social class,* but to refer to politicians collectively. A common example of this use of **classe** is in **a classe médica** *(the medical profession).*

Uma herdade. This term for a large farm is used particularly in the Alentejo. It once meant *an inheritance.* In English, the word *estate* is still used to refer both to land and to what is inherited.

For a fuller account of the complex issue of land in Portugal before and after the 25th of April 1974, see:

Gallagher, Tom   *Portugal — a twentieth-century interpretation*
Manchester University Press, 1983.

Robinson, Richard   *Contemporary Portugal — a history*
Allen and Unwin, 1979.

THE ALENTEJO AND THE 25 APRIL (II)

Q: *Was land of yours occupied too?*

A: Everything that belonged to my father was occupied. In July '75, September '75, October '75, everything that he had was all occupied. Something did remain unoccupied, which were properties of mine that had been bought — acquired — a short time before, and where there wasn't so much wealth as there was in the other ones. Those belonging to my father, which had quite a lot of cattle, quite a lot of produce in store, good implements and tractors... well those are the ones that were occupied. The procedure was precisely to occupy what was in production, and not what was abandoned — the opposite of what the politicians of the time said, and the MFA itself, the Armed Forces Movement, for they were working together.

Q: *And what did you do when they occupied your land?*

A: Practically I did nothing. I didn't fight. I didn't fight physically, because it was impossible to fight. It was impossible at the time to fight because the military were occupying the land, with military vehicles, with G-3s, with guns, accompanying the workers in their occupation of the estates. This was the reality of the Alentejo. When it's said that it was the workers who did the occupying, it wasn't the workers. The workers were incited to occupy by civilian political forces and by left-wing military.

9   A GUITARRA PORTUGUESA

Turning from rural to urban life, we asked the musician Pedro Caldeira Cabral to describe the characteristics of **a guitarra** — not to be confused with the 'Spanish' guitar, which the Portuguese call **a viola** — and to talk about its place in Portuguese culture. He sees both the instrument and the music associated with it as bridges between popular and 'high' culture. His final comments refer to the function of songs, particularly in the 1960s and early 1970s, as a means of protest against the authoritarian values of the Salazar regime.

Q: *Pedro, como é que se podem descrever as características da guitarra portuguesa?*

A: A guitarra portuguesa tem características muito originais: o facto de ter cordas metálicas, de ter cordas duplas, e de ter este tipo de cavalete e este tipo de forma periforme, digamos assim. Este instrumento está relacionado com a cítara do Renascimento, que foi, digamos, o seu antepassado mais longínquo, que tinha também estas características. Mas, para além disso, existe uma técnica especial de utilização da guitarra que nós chamamos de dedilho, que só é utilizada com este instrumento. E depois, o próprio tipo de música que se criou para este instrumento é de facto, também, qualquer coisa original e diferente daquilo que se faz noutros países.

Q: *E dentro da cultura portuguesa, que lugar é que ocupa? Qual é a função da guitarra portuguesa relacionada à cultura portuguesa?*

A: Bom, eu penso que a guitarra portuguesa é um instrumento popular. É um instrumento fundamentalmente ligado à tradição oral, mas é um instrumento urbano também. É um instrumento que só se pode compreender num quadro urbano; não é um instrumento rural. Mesmo como peça de violaria, podemos encontrar características que combinam conhecimentos cultos com as tradições, digamos, populares de construção. Este sistema, por exemplo, de afinação, que é um sistema extremamente preciso, aparentemente foi inventado por um relojoeiro no século XVIII. É um sistema que permite uma afinação perfeitamente rigorosa — o que é um sinal duma certa inteligência, que é, enfim, um sinal dum instrumento culto. Mas, depois, encontram-se outros tipos de combinações, como a ornamentação por exemplo, que estão intimamente ligadas às tradições populares. É nitidamente um instrumento com uma forma e com um tipo popular.

Portanto, é fundamentalmente um instrumento de características populares. Mas, a certa altura, pelo tipo de gente em que foi especialmente cultivado, invadiu o terreno das salas de concerto. E portanto a música que hoje se toca na guitarra portuguesa — que eu toco, que o Carlos Paredes toca, por exemplo — é uma música que estabelece uma ponte entre a música popular e a música culta. E nesse sentido a guitarra portuguesa, e a música da guitarra portuguesa, aparece ligada a estudantes, aparece ligada a movimentos de contestação, inclusive da resistência cultural, se quiseres, numa época em que os valores populares eram rejeitados e se criaram determinados esterótipos culturais que os substituíam.

Language notes

1 A striking feature of the language here is the quantity of passive constructions, of both types. The passive tends to be used for making impersonal, objective statements, hence its use in text 6 and here. First, the passive using **ser** with the past participle:

é utilizado *is used*

foi { **inventado** / **cultivado** } *was* { *invented* / *cultivated* }

eram rejeitados *were rejected*

With the above type of passive, it is possible to continue the phrase, using **por...** *(by...)*, and to say by whom something was used/ invented/cultivated, etc. However, the type of passive that uses **se** obscures more completely the person(s) responsible for what is/was done. So the use of this passive, in particular, corresponds to the impersonal, objective quality of this text.

o tipo de música que se criou *the type of music that was created*
aquilo que se faz *what (that which) is done*
só se pode compreender *it can only be understood*
encontram-se outros tipos *other types are found*
a música que hoje se toca *the music which is played today*
em que... se criaram *in which certain stereotypes*
   determinados esterótipos *were created*

2 **Se quiseres** *(if you like, if you wish)* is the future subjunctive (the familiar **tu** form). See **Grammar 9.15**. Like the word **digamos** *(let's say, so to speak)*, which occurs several times, **se quiseres** is used partly as a gap-filler, to give the speaker time to think of what he is going to say next. However, like their counterparts in English, both expressions also function here as a form of politeness, a hesitation about being dogmatic, which counterbalances the impersonal tone conveyed by the passive.

THE PORTUGUESE GUITAR

Q: *Pedro, how can the characteristics of the Portuguese guitar be described?*

A: The Portuguese guitar has very original characteristics: the fact that it has metal strings, double strings, and this type of bridge and this kind of pear-shaped form, let's say. This instrument is related to the Renaissance zither, which was, one might say, its most distant ancestor and which also had these characteristics. But, apart from that, there is a special technique in using the guitar that we call plucking, which is only used with this instrument. And then the kind of music itself that was created for this instrument is in fact also something original and different from what is done in other countries.

Q: *And within Portuguese culture, what place does it have? What is the function of the Portuguese guitar in relation to Portuguese culture?*

A: Well, I think the Portuguese guitar is an instrument of the people. It's an instrument fundamentally linked to oral tradition, but it's an urban instrument too. It's an instrument that can only be understood in an urban context; it's not a rural instrument. Even as a stringed instrument, we can find features that combine sophisticated knowledge with, let's say, popular traditions of instrument-making. This system of tuning, for example, which is a very precise system, was apparently invented by a watch-maker in the eighteenth century. It's a system which makes possible perfectly accurate tuning — something which indicates a certain refinement, which in fact indicates a sophisticated instrument. But then there are other kinds of combination, such as the ornamentation for example, which are intimately related to popular traditions. It is clearly an instrument of a shape and type that belong to popular tradition.

So it's fundamentally an instrument that has popular features. But, at a certain point in time, through the kind of people among whom it was particularly cultivated, it invaded the terrain of the concert hall. And so the music that is played today on the Portuguese guitar — the music that I play, that Carlos Paredes* plays, for example — is music that establishes a bridge between the popular and classical. And in this sense the Portuguese guitar and Portuguese guitar music are associated with students, with protest movements, cultural resistance if you like, in a period in which the values of ordinary people were being rejected and certain cultural stereotypes were created to replace them.

*Carlos Paredes, the leading
Portuguese guitarist, composed
and performed the theme
music for the television series,
Discovering Portuguese.

The major form of decorative art in Portugal has been the ornamental tile, **o azulejo,** which you come across in every type of building, from churches and stately homes to railway-stations and cafés. We asked Rafael Calado, Director of the **Museu do Azulejo** in Lisbon, why this art form is so important in Portugal. His answer refers to the period 1580-1640, when Portugal was under Spanish rule. Both these dates are very significant for the Portuguese: the loss of independence in 1580 coincided with the death of Camões, and the year 1580 has sometimes been regarded as marking the end of the golden age of Portuguese history. 1640 was the year of the restoration of independence, commemorated by the name of the Lisbon square — **a Praça dos Restauradores.**

Q: *Podia-me dizer porque é que os azulejos parecem ser tão importantes para os portugueses?*

A: Os azulejos são realmente uma forma de expressão nas artes ornamentais extremamente importante para nós na medida em que preencheu, num período sério dessas mesmas artes ornamentais

Azulejos
*in the Miradouro
de Santa Luzia, Lisbon*

(ou seja, no período barroco), uma área através da qual nos permitiu acompanhar a estética contemporânea – ou seja, durante o período da ocupação filipina. Portanto, quando Filipe II de Espanha começou a construir a grande capital do seu império – Madrid – Portugal, que era um país que estava subjugado à coroa de Espanha, perdeu toda a possibilidade, como país dominado, de evoluir do ponto de vista artístico. Era um país em que não se construía, em que as coisas sumptuárias não faziam sentido: estava completamente vencido. Então os portugueses de repente sentiram essa necessidade de acompanhar esse movimento estético de toda a atitude filosófica do barroco, através dos meios que tinham à sua disposição. E assim viemos parar ao azulejo, não por opção mas por recurso. Portanto o azulejo veio a substituir a tapeçaria, a pintura mural e outras formas de arte sumptuária. Portanto é uma forma modesta que nós utilizámos para resolver o assunto. Ao longo de sessenta anos, que foi o período de domínio filipino em Portugal, o azulejo radica-se profundamente no gosto do povo, e dissemina-se por todo o país. Portanto, ao fim de sessenta anos o país se torna independente e passa a ter rei próprio. Nesta altura o azulejo já estava profundamente radicado no gosto dos portugueses, através de gerações – quer dizer, da utilização desse mesmo azulejo. Daí para a frente, evoluiu até aos nossos dias.

Language notes

1 This speaker is relating quite a complex history, so he needs to use expressions which make it clear what happened when, and what the situation was at certain points in time:

num no durante o	} período...	in a in the during a	} period...
ao longo de ao fim de	} sessenta anos	for (during a period of) after	} sixty years

nesta altura...   *at / by this time*
daí para a frente...   *from then onwards*

2 The fact that the speaker is giving a history also means that this text provides plenty of examples of the use of the preterite and imperfect. Here is just one of them to remind you of the distinction between 'event' (preterite) and 'situation' (imperfect):

quando Felipe II começou a construir a grande capital do seu império, Portugal, que era um país que estava subjugado..., perdeu toda a possibilidade...

3 Towards the end, he briefly uses the present tense to narrate what happened in the past. This use of the present tense is mentioned in **Grammar 9.5**.

4 Apart from the time expressions, other connecting phrases are:

na medida em que   *to the extent to which* (**uma medida** is *a measure*)
ou seja   *or rather, that is*

TILES

Q: *Could you tell me why* **azulejos** *seem to be so important to the Portuguese?*

A: **Azulejos** are a form of expression in the decorative arts which is really extremely important to us in that, during a period which is significant in these decorative arts (that is, the Baroque period), this form of expression filled an area through which we were enabled to keep up with the contemporary aesthetic movement — that is, during the period of the Philipine occupation. So, when Philip II of Spain began to build the great capital of his empire — Madrid — Portugal, which was a country that was subject to the crown of Spain, lost all possibility, as a dominated country, of developing from the artistic point of view. It was a country in which building didn't happen, in which luxury items had no place: it was completely conquered. So the Portuguese suddenly felt the need to keep up with this aesthetic movement, the whole philosophical attitude of the Baroque, through the means they had at their disposal. And so we came to use the **azulejo,** not by choice but as the only resort. So the **azulejo** came to replace the tapestry, the mural and other forms of luxury art. So it's a modest form, which we used to solve the matter. In the course of sixty years, which was the period of Philipine domination in Portugal, the **azulejo** becomes deeply rooted in public taste, and spreads throughout the whole country. So, after sixty years the country becomes independent and comes to have a king of its own. By this time the **azulejo** was deeply rooted in Portuguese taste, through several generations — that is, of use of the **azulejo.** From then on, it has evolved up to the present day.

11 A FUNDAÇÃO GULBENKIAN E A ARTE PORTUGUESA

Still in the domain of the visual arts, we asked Pedro Támen of the Calouste Gulbenkian Foundation (and, incidentally, a distinguished poet) to explain its function in the development of what has been in recent years a lively artistic world in Portugal. Our second question — can one talk about a specifically Portuguese art? — is more difficult to answer, and takes us back to the question of national identity. After pointing out the international character of contemporary painting, Pedro Támen risks at least one generalisation: that Portuguese art, and indeed Portuguese culture in general, shows lyrical rather than dramatic qualities.

Q: *Qual é a função da Gulbenkian quanto à promoção e desenvolvimento da arte portuguesa dentro de Portugal?*

A: A arte é um dos quatro fins da Fundação, tal como o Sr. Calouste Gulbenkian a criou. E desde o princípio, desde que a Fundação começou a existir há trinta anos, tem procurado atingir esse fim, e de diversas maneiras (...) Existem dois museus na Fundação, um que alberga a colecção do Sr. Calouste Gulbenkian, e outro — este Centro de Arte Moderna em que estamos, construído em grande parte com uma colecção adquirida aos próprios artistas. Esses museus são já uma maneira de incentivar e de ajudar a arte em Portugal. E a arte são os artistas, porque os artistas é quem a fazem. Não é uma abstracção. Mas por outro lado, desde o princípio, a Fundação tem desenvolvido

The Gulbenkian Ballet

um programa de bolsas de estudo, que permite o aperfeiçoamento dos artistas, quer em Portugal, quer no estrangeiro, noutros meios artísticos. E tem todo um programa de subsídios que lhes permitem trabalhar, fazer exposições, mostrar a sua produção (…)

Q: *Há arte portuguesa, mesmo portuguesa?*

A: É uma pergunta difícil… No fundo, perguntar se há arte portuguesa é perguntar qual é a identidade do português, relativamente a outros povos. E corremos aí sempre o risco da generalização e da abstracção. No entanto, eu penso que uma ou outra característica se pode sempre discernir ao longo da nossa produção artística e literária, e portanto também nas artes plásticas. Mas hoje, em que talvez mais do que nunca, com a facilidade de contactos, hoje um artista em Lisboa tem muito mais facilidade de estar ao corrente do que estão a fazer os artistas em Munique ou em Londres. Com esta facilidade de contactos, com esta instantaneidade do conhecimento, há naturalmente muito mais facilidade ou risco de a arte se tornar uniforme, ou de se mover dentro de padrões uniformes — o que complica ainda mais a questão. No entanto, eu penso que mesmo nos artistas portugueses mais aparentemente identificáveis com as modas ou as correntes artísticas de outros países, mesmo nesses artistas eu penso que há sempre qualquer coisa, ou há quase sempre qualquer coisa de português. Dizer o que é que há de português naquilo é que é o mais difícil. Voltamos sempre à mesma dificuldade. Mas se quisesse que eu resumisse isso numa palavra, eu diria que é uma tendência lírica versus uma tendência dramática — que é, por exemplo, muito mais espanhola do que portuguesa. Tem que ver também com características gerais da nossa cultura, da nossa literatura por exemplo, cujo vector fundamental — eu me atrevo a dizer — é justamente o lírico.

Language notes

1   In the reply to the first question, there are two further examples of the compound perfect tense (see text 1, note 3 and **Grammar 9.9**):

desde que a Fundação começou a existir…, tem procurado atingir esse fim
desde o princípio, a Fundação tem desenvolvido um programa de bolsas de estudo

The use of this tense implies that these activities are still going on.   149

2 Given the difficulty of the second question, the speaker is cautious in his reply, hence a number of expressions, some of which you are familiar with, for qualifying what he is saying:

no fundo *basically*
no entanto *nevertheless*
mas *but*
talvez *perhaps*
quase sempre *almost always*

3 On the use of **estar** followed by **a** and the infinitive of another verb, see **Grammar 9.5**.

o que estão a fazer *what they are doing*

4 You will find a lot of the vocabulary in this text fairly straightforward, but it is worth drawing attention to a few words and phrases:

ainda mais *even more*
tem que ver com... *it has to do with...*
se quisesse que eu resumisse *if you wanted me to sum up* (imperfect subjunctive)
atrever-se a *to dare to*

THE GULBENKIAN FOUNDATION AND PORTUGUESE ART

Q: *What is the function of the Gulbenkian as regards the promotion and development of Portuguese art within Portugal?*

A: Art is one of the four aims of the Foundation, as Mr. Calouste Gulbenkian created it. And from the beginning, since the Foundation came into existence thirty years ago, it has tried to achieve this aim, and in a variety of ways (...) There are two museums in the Foundation, one which houses Mr. Calouste Gulbenkian's collection, and another one — this Modern Art Centre where we are, built up largely with a collection acquired from the artists themselves. These museums are already a way of giving an incentive and of helping art in Portugal. And art is the artists, because it's the artists who make it. It's not an abstraction. But also, from the beginning, the Foundation has developed a programme of scholarships which allows artists to develop their talents, either in Portugal or abroad, in other artistic environments. And it has a whole programme of grants which allow them to work, to put on exhibitions, to show the work they produce (...)

Q: *Is there such a thing as Portuguese art, really Portuguese?*

A: It's a difficult question... Basically, asking if there is Portuguese art is the same as asking what is the identity of the Portuguese, in relation to other nations. And here we run the risk of generalisations and abstractions. Nevertheless, I think that one or two characteristics can always be found throughout our artistic and literary production, and therefore in the plastic arts too. But today, when perhaps more than ever, with easy communications, today an artist in Lisbon finds it much easier to be in touch with what artists are doing in Munich or in London. With this easy contact, with this immediate awareness, there is naturally much more possibility or risk of art becoming uniform, or of keeping within uniform patterns — which complicates the question even more. Nevertheless, I think that even in the Portuguese artists most apparently identifiable with the fashions or artistic trends of other countries, even in these artists I think there is always something, or almost always something Portuguese. To say what it is that's Portuguese in all that, that's the most difficult thing. We always come back to the same difficulty. But if you wanted me to sum this up in one word, I'd say that it's a tendency towards the lyrical rather than the dramatic — which is something much more Spanish, for example, than Portuguese. It also has to do with certain general characteristics of our culture, of our literature for example, of which the fundamental tendency — I would go so far as to say — is precisely lyrical.

12 A LÍNGUA PORTUGUESA

Finally, if you need encouragement to continue with Portuguese, President Soares gives you one good reason why the language is important! (He refers at the beginning to his exile: under the Salazar regime, Dr. Soares was a prominent opposition lawyer, who defended people accused of 'political offences' — hence his exile.)

Try listening to the cassette before you read the text, and see if you can find the answers to the following questions. Then check your answers in the Portuguese and/or English texts.

How many people in the world today speak Portuguese?
Which Portuguese-speaking areas of the world are mentioned?
How many Portuguese-speakers are there likely to be by the end of the century?
Where does Portuguese come in the order of most widely spoken languages?
Which languages does he mention which are more widely spoken than Portuguese?
Which language does he mention which is less widely spoken than Portuguese?

Q: *O Senhor Presidente acha que é importante os estrangeiros aprenderem a falar português antes de virem a Portugal?*

A: Eu acho que sim, e tenho autoridade para lhe falar nisso porque eu fui... quando estava exilado... fui professor de português em várias universidades — em Rennes, e em Paris na Sorbonne. E na altura dizia aos meus alunos, que eram estrangeiros naturalmente, franceses, dizia-lhes que o português era uma língua mais importante que a própria língua francesa, porque é mais falada no mundo e vai ser no futuro muito mais falada do que o francês. Nós neste momento temos 150 milhões de seres humanos que falam português — com o Brasil, com a África, com certas comunidades que existem ainda na Índia, em Macau, 151 na Indonésia e Timor particularmente. E por outro lado, com a evolução demográfica, nós pensamos que no final deste século 200 milhões de seres humanos falarão o português, o que significa que nós somos a quinta língua mais falada do mundo — mais falada do que a língua francesa. Evidentemente, os ingleses têm a língua que é a mais falada de todo o Universo, mas os espanhóis têm uma língua que é muito falada também, que é mais falada do que a nossa. Mas Portugal, sendo um pequeno país, é um país muito bem colocado nesse conjunto de seres humanos que falam a nossa língua, graças em particular a esse portentoso país que é o Brasil.

Language notes

1   The question contains two more examples of the 'personal' infinitive (see text 3, note 3; text 4, note 1; **Grammar 9.14**).

2   Since the speaker is talking about the relative position of Portuguese in the world, the text illustrates the way you make comparisons using **do que** (see Unit 5, section 27):

$$\text{mais} \left\{ \begin{array}{l} \text{importante} \\ \text{falada} \end{array} \right\} \text{do que} \left\{ \begin{array}{l} \text{a própria língua francesa} \\ \text{o francês} \\ \text{a língua francesa} \\ \text{a nossa} \end{array} \right.$$

In this type of comparison **do** is occasionally omitted.

THE PORTUGUESE LANGUAGE

Q: *Do you think, Mr. President, that it's important for foreigners to learn to speak Portuguese before they come to Portugal?*

A: I think so, and I have some authority to speak about this to you because I was... when I was exiled... I was a Portuguese teacher at various universities — in Rennes, and in Paris at the Sorbonne. And at that time I used to tell my students, who were foreigners naturally, French, I used to say to them that Portuguese was a more important language than the French language itself, because it is more widely spoken in the world, and in the future it's going to be much more widely spoken than French. We at this moment have 150 million people who speak Portuguese — what with Brazil, with Africa, with certain communities that still exist in India, in Macau, in Indonesia and particularly Timor. And also, with the growth in population, we think that by the end of the century 200 million people will speak Portuguese, which means that we are the fifth most widely spoken language in the world — more widely spoken than French. Obviously, the English have the most widely spoken language in the entire world, but the Spanish have a language that is very widely spoken too, more widely spoken than ours. But Portugal, although it's a small country, is very well placed within this community of people who speak our language, thanks particularly to that prodigious country, Brazil.

Reference Section

PRONUNCIATION

The best way to achieve good pronunciation in Portuguese is to practise with the cassettes, listening carefully and trying to reproduce the sounds you hear. The following is intended only as a brief guide to some of the more obvious features.

The Portuguese examples below are recorded on your cassette. Bold type is used to draw your attention to the relevant part of each example.

Stress

1 Words which end in **a**, **e**, **o**, **am**, **em**, or **s** are usually stressed on the last syllable but one: **bi**ca, **tar**de, ga**ro**to, de**se**jam, van**ta**gem, portu**gue**ses.

The above endings may follow immediately after a vowel. If so, the vowel usually forms the stressed syllable: pastela**ri**a, que**ri**am, pe**sso**a, conti**nu**a.

2 Words with endings other than those in 1 are usually stressed on the final syllable: a**qui**, natu**ral**, fa**lar**, as**sim**.

3 Exceptions to the above rules are usually indicated by a written accent on the stressed syllable: far**má**cia, a**mên**doa, es**pé**cie, **pró**ximo, tam**bém**, portu**guês**.

Vowels

As in English, the pronunciation of vowels in Portuguese often depends on whether or not the syllable is stressed.

stressed	a usually as in c**a**sa, c**a**rro, f**a**lo; but when followed by **m**, **n**, or **nh** as in c**a**ma, **A**na, b**a**nho
unstressed	a usually as in bic**a**, p**a**rtir, f**a**lar
stressed	e usually either as in empr**e**go, m**e**sa, c**e**sto; or as in past**e**l, ab**e**rto, compl**e**to
unstressed	e usually as in p**e**dir, s**e**, noit**e** (barely sounded at the end of a word)
stressed *unstressed* }	i as in b**i**ca, aqu**i**, moçamb**i**cano
stressed	o either as in b**o**lo, gar**o**to, d**o**ce; or as in h**o**mem, n**o**sso, m**o**ra
unstressed	o usually as in g**o**star, c**o**lega, j**o**rnal
stressed *unstressed* }	u as in c**u**sta, c**u**star, s**u**bo, s**u**bir

154

Combinations of two vowels

In the combinations **ai, au, ei, eu, iu, oi, ou** and **ui**, the stress is usually on the first of the two vowels (mais, mau, seis, meu, partiu, dois, pouco, Rui) unless a written accent indicates otherwise (país, aí).

However, when any of these combinations is followed by **m, n,** or **r,** it is usually the second vowel that is stressed: Coimbra, ainda, sair.

Nasal sounds

See Unit 1, section 3.

Consonants

Many consonants in Portuguese are similar to their equivalents in English. For those that differ most from English, see Unit 1, section 5 and Unit 2, section 12.

BRAZILIAN PORTUGUESE

The Portuguese you have learned in this course is European Portuguese. As with English, there are, of course, different varieties of Portuguese. Within Portugal there are regional variations in the language, especially in pronunciation, and such variations are even more obvious between the different parts of the Portuguese-speaking world. It is beyond the scope of this course to deal with all these differences, but a brief word about Brazilian Portuguese may be helpful.

The gap between European and Brazilian Portuguese is similar to that between British and American English. There are a few differences in grammar, most obviously in the use of pronouns and in the use of some verb tenses, notably the 'present continuous' *(I am... ing):* where the Portuguese would say, for example, **Estou a falar português,** the Brazilians say **Estou falando português.**

In the written language, there are differences in the use of accents, and also minor variations in spelling. For example, words containing **cç, ct, pç** and **pt** are written in Brazil without the first consonant, e.g. **ação** (Portugal: **acção**), **fato** (**facto**), **exato** (**exacto**). However, you will not find it difficult to adapt to written Brazilian Portuguese. Especially in more formal kinds of writing, the differences between the two varieties are fairly minor.

In the spoken language, there are differences in pronunciation. Brazilian vowels are much more 'open', and you may find you can hear them more clearly. However, perhaps the most dramatic difference is the Brazilian pronunciation (especially in the states of Rio, São Paulo and Minas Gerais) of **d** and **t** when they occur before an **i**, or an **e** sounding like an **i**. In these two situations, **d** sounds like the **j** in John, and **t** like the **ch** in Charles. This may seem a small detail, but until you get used to it the effect is startling. Another striking difference in Brazilian Portuguese is that **r** often sounds rather like an English **h**, for example when it occurs at the beginning of a word or as a double **rr**. It doesn't take long to adjust to decoding these sounds, and you may in fact find Brazilian easier to understand than Portuguese. As an illustration, your cassette contains a passage adapted from a 1984 issue of the Brazilian magazine **'Veja',** followed by a translation. The reader is from São Paulo.

Novo sabor: os baianos descobrem o suco de cacau.

Os baianos, que o cultivam há mais de dois séculos, achavam que o cacau já havia esgotado todo o seu rol de utilizações. Estavam enganados. Há pouco tempo, eles próprios descobriram que a polpa desse fruto também se presta à fabricação de um saboroso e nutritivo suco. Batida com água e açúcar, resulta numa bebida leitosa, muito refrescante, que se assemelha na aparência ao suco de fruta-do-conde. Seu sabor, no entanto, é completamente diferente de todos os refrescos conhecidos e nem de longe lembra o mais nobre produto do cacau — o chocolate. O fato é que o suco de cacau se transformou numa verdadeira mania em Salvador e, dali, já está decolando para outras cidades brasileiras. 'É uma das bebidas mais gostosas e mais genuinamente brasileiras que já provei', garante o artista plástico Carybé.

Em Salvador, pode-se tomar cerca de quarenta tipos diferentes de sucos, O de cacau, no entanto, é de longe o mais consumido.

New flavour: the Bahians discover cocoa juice.

The Bahians, who have been cultivating cocoa for over two centuries, thought that its range of possible uses had already been exhausted. They were wrong. Not long ago, they themselves discovered that the pulp of this fruit can be used in the preparation of a delicious and nourishing juice. Beaten with water and sugar it turns into a very refreshing milky drink that is similar in appearance to custard apple juice. Its taste, however, is completely unlike any known drink and does not even remotely remind you of the noblest cocoa product — chocolate. The fact is that cocoa juice has become a real craze in Salvador and, from there, it is taking off to other Brazilian cities. 'It's one of the most delicious and most genuinely Brazilian drinks I've ever tasted', assures artist Carybé.

In Salvador, you can have nearly fifty different kinds of juice. Cocoa juice, however, is by far the most widely consumed.

There are also differences in vocabulary between European and Brazilian Portuguese, some due to the influence of Amerindian languages — especially in place-names. Other terms used in Brazil result from the fact that it is a tropical country and has names for plants and animals, for example, which simply do not exist in Europe. Sometimes these terms mean little to a European, even when translated. Often, however, the differences in vocabulary are in areas of everyday life. Here are some examples:

Portugal	Brazil	
a alcunha	o apelido	*nick-name*
o ananás	o abacaxi	*pineapple*
o apelido	o sobrenome	*surname*
o autocarro	o ônibus	*bus*
a bica, o café	o cafezinho	*(small) black coffee*
a bicha	a fila	*queue*
o bilhete	a passagem	*ticket*
a bilheteira	a bilheteria	*ticket-office*
a boleia	a carona	*lift (by car)*
o cachorro	o cachorrinho	*puppy*
o caminho de ferro	a estrada de ferro	*railway*
a camisa de dormir	a camisola	*nightdress*
a camisola	o suéter	*sweater, pullover*

Portugal	Brazil	
o cão	o cachorro	*dog*
a carta de condução	a carteira de habilitação	*driving-licence*
a casa de banho	o banheiro	*bathroom, toilet*
a chávena	a xícara	*cup*
o comboio	o trem	*train*
a constipação	o resfriado	*cold, chill*
estar constipado, a	estar resfriado, a	*to have a cold*
as cuecas	as calcinhas, a calça	*panties*
o eléctrico	o bonde	*tram*
a ementa, a lista	o menu, o cardápio	*menu*
o empregado	o garção	*waiter*
a erva	o capim	*grass*
a esquadra (da polícia)	a delegacia de polícia	*police station*
o facto	o fato	*fact*
o fato	o terno	*suit*
o frigorífico	a geladeira	*fridge*
a frutaria	a quitanda	*fruit shop*
o galão	a média	*(large) white coffee*
guiar, conduzir	dirigir	*to drive*
impedido	ocupado	*engaged (telephone)*
uma imperial, um fino	um chope	*a draught beer*
o livro de cheques	o talão de cheques	*cheque book*
meter gasolina	pôr gasolina	*fill up with petrol*
o metro	o metrô	*underground (railway)*
a montra	a vitrina	*shop window*
a paragem	a parada, o ponto	*stop (bus, tram)*
o pequeno almoço	café da manhã	*breakfast*
o polícia	o polícia, o policial	*policeman*
a praça de táxi	o ponto de táxi	*taxi-stand*
o rés-do-chão	o andar térreo	*ground floor*
seis	meia (i.e. meia dúzia)	*six (e.g. in giving a phone number)*
a senhora	a senhorinha, a senhorita	*Miss*
o sumo	o suco	*juice*
o talho	o açougue	*butcher's*
o travão	o freio	*brake*

GRAMMAR

1 Introduction

The main aim of this section of the book is to provide a brief summary of the language presented in Part I. However, the following pages also include some aspects not covered in Units 1-6, or touched on very briefly. This extra material is intended to help you develop your Portuguese further by using the Grammar section together with the Anthology in Part II.

In order to understand the grammar of Portuguese it is useful to bear in mind a few basic principles.

Unlike English, Portuguese nouns (the names of people and things) belong to one of two conventional categories: they are either masculine or feminine (their gender).

Like English, they are also either singular or plural (their number).

The gender and number of a noun affect other words associated with it, which must agree — that is, they must have the appropriate ending to show their connection with the noun.

Agreement exists to a limited extent in English, in relation to verbs (words of doing, thinking, feeling, being). You say, for example, *I do* but *he/she does*. In Portuguese, the system of agreement is much more extensive. For example, it includes adjectives, and the words for *a* and *the*, e.g. **o vinho branco** (white wine); **as casas brancas** (the white houses).

Agreement also extends to verbs, which must agree with their subject (the person or thing doing the action). The form of the verb therefore indicates to a large extent whether the subject is *I* or *we* (first person), *you* (second person), *he/she/it* or *they* (third person). This is why you usually omit the words for *I, you* etc.

Unlike English, Portuguese has various ways of saying *'you'*. As well as a second person form (**tu**), there is also a third person form: **você** or **o senhor/a senhora**. The circumstances in which you use **o senhor/a senhora**, **você** and **tu** are explained in Unit 2, section 3.

2 Articles

The form of an article depends on whether the word that follows is masculine or feminine, and whether it is singular or plural.

2.1 The indefinite article *(a, an)*

masculine	*feminine*
um	uma

2.2 Contracted forms

Where **um** or **uma** would follow **de** or **em**, the words combine as follows:

with:	masculine	feminine	
de *(of, from)*	dum	duma	*of a, from a*
em *(in, on)*	num	numa	*in a, on a*

Written Portuguese is slightly inconsistent here: **num** and **numa** are always written in the contracted form, but you will frequently find **de um** and **de uma**, written as separate words.

2.3 The definite article *(the)*

	masculine	feminine
singular	o	a
plural	os	as

2.4 Contracted forms

Where **o**, **os** or **as** would follow **a**, **de**, **em** or **por**, the words combine as follows:

with:		masculine	feminine	
a *(to)*	*singular*	ao	à	*to the*
	plural	aos	às	
de *(of, from)*	*singular*	do	da	*of/from the*
	plural	dos	das	
em *(in, on)*	*singular*	no	na	*in/on the*
	plural	nos	nas	
por *(through, for, because of)*	*singular*	pelo	pela	*through* (etc.) *the*
	plural	pelos	pelas	

2.5 Uses of the definite and indefinite articles

In both Portuguese and English the choice of one or other article, or their omission, depends on how general or specific the statement is. However, the two languages do not always coincide in the way this is done. The following is a rough guide; the order of the examples goes from the more general to the more specific.

In referring to the whole of a category, to a concept or an abstraction, the two languages differ: in Portuguese you use **o** or **a**, in English you omit the article.

O homem põe e Deus dispõe   *Man proposes, God disposes*
A liberdade é fundamental   *Freedom is fundamental*

In defining someone as a member of a general category, the two languages again differ: in Portuguese you omit the article, in English you say *a...*

Ela é médica   *She is a doctor*
Sou turista   *I'm a tourist*

In referring to some of a category, without being specific, the two languages are the same: neither uses the article.

Está a procurar trabalho   *He's looking for work*
Quer vinho ou cerveja?   *Do you want wine or beer?*

In referring to one of a category, not unique but singled out for attention, the two languages are the same: both use the indefinite article.

Visitámos um museu   *We visited a museum*
Era uma vez um rapaz...   *Once upon a time there was a boy...*
Quer uma cerveja?   *Do you want a beer?*

However, in referring to several of a category, singled out for attention, the two languages have different ways of conveying distinctions of meaning. Portuguese uses either **uns/umas** or **alguns/algumas** to make a distinction which in English is conveyed by stress. (In the examples, the words stressed in English are underlined.)

Vimos uns soldados na rua   *We saw some <u>soldiers</u> in the street*
Alguns engenheiros   <u>*Some*</u> *engineers have solved*
  resolveram este problema   *this problem*

In referring to a clearly specified member of a category — unique in the context, or previously mentioned — both languages are the same: both use the definite article.

O café é muito bom   *The coffee is very good*
O homem entrou na casa   *The man went into the house*

3   **Demonstratives** *(this, that)*

3.1   Portuguese has two words for *'that'*. **Esse** is used to refer to what is close to or associated with the person being spoken to; **aquele** for what is remote from both the speaker and the person addressed.

Except in their neuter form, the demonstratives agree in gender and number with what they refer to.

masculine	feminine	neuter	
este	esta	isto	*this, this one*
esse	essa	isso	*that, that one* (near you)
aquele	aquela	aquilo	*that, that one* (over there)

To form the plurals of the masculine and feminine forms, add **s**.

3.2 Contracted forms

Where **este**, **esse** or **aquele** would follow **de** or **em**, the words combine as follows:

masculine	feminine	neuter	
deste	desta	disto	*of this, of this one*
desse	dessa	disso	*of that, of that one*
daquele	daquela	daquilo	*of that, of that one*
neste	nesta	nisto	*in this, in this one*
nesse	nessa	nisso	*in that, in that one*
naquele	naquela	naquilo	*in that, in that one*

Where **aquele** would follow **a**, the words combine as below. The written accent indicates the change in sound resulting from the contraction of the two vowels (**a** + **a**).

masculine	feminine	neuter	
àquele	àquela	àquilo	*to that, to that one*

3.3 Uses

The masculine and feminine forms are used as adjectives:

Vai por esta rua — *Go along this street*
Gosto desse vestido — *I like that dress*
Moramos naquela casa — *We live in that house*

And as pronouns:

Vai por esta — *Go along this one*
Gosto desse — *I like that one*
Moramos naquela — *We live in that one*

The neuter forms refer not to a specific person or thing, but to a whole situation that has been referred to or is understood in the conversation or text. They sometimes occur with **tudo** *(everything)*.

Isto é impossível! — *This is impossible!*
Tudo aquilo é muito complicado — *The whole thing is very complicated*
Quem disse isso? — *Who said that?*

4 Possessives

4.1 In Portuguese, unlike English, the possessives (*my, mine; your, yours* etc.) agree with the thing(s) possessed.

	masculine		feminine	
	singular	*plural*	*singular*	*plural*
eu nós	o meu o nosso	os meus os nossos	a minha a nossa	as minhas as nossas
tu vocês	o teu o vosso	os teus os vossos	a tua a vossa	as tuas as vossas
ele / ela você o senhor a senhora eles / elas vocês os senhores as senhoras	o seu	os seus	a sua	as suas

4.2 Since **o seu, a sua** and their plural forms can mean *his, hers, yours* or *theirs*, there is an alternative form which is used if there might otherwise be any ambiguity. This alternative form is like saying *the… of him, the… of you* etc.

o(s) / a(s)…	dele	*his…*
	dela	*her…*
	deles delas	*their…*
	do senhor da senhora dos senhores das senhoras	*your…*

4.3 Uses

Possessives are used either as adjectives *(my…, your…)* or as pronouns *(mine, yours)*.

As adjectives, those listed in 4.1 normally come before the noun; those listed in 4.2 always follow the noun.

a nossa casa	*our house*
os meus livros	*my books*
o passaporte do senhor	*your passport*
o carro deles	*their car*
os pais delas	*their parents*

163

With **um** + noun the possessive follows the noun, and corresponds to the English *of mine, of yours* etc.

um amigo meu   *a friend of mine*

The definite article is omitted in phrases of the type **Este dinheiro é meu** *(This money is mine)*.

5   Nouns

5.1   Gender (masculine / feminine)

Nouns that denote male members of a species are masculine, those that denote females are feminine, e.g. **um homem, uma mulher**.

In all other areas, the gender of nouns is arbitrary and not easy to predict. However, there are some fairly general patterns.

Nouns ending in **-o** are usually masculine (though not necessarily if they end in **-ão**), e.g. **um garoto, o vinho, o almoço**.

Nouns ending as follows are feminine:

-a: **uma casa, a cerveja, a comida**. Common exceptions are: **o dia, o guia, o mapa**; nouns of Greek origin ending in **-ma** (**um telegrama, um programa, o sistema**); some words for categories of people, if they refer to a man (**um lojista, um jornalista, um turista**).

-ção, -são, -stão, -gião: **a estação, a televisão, uma sugestão, uma região**.

-dade, -gem, -ie, -tude: **a cidade, uma viagem, uma espécie, a saúde**.

5.2   Plurals

To form the plural of singular nouns ending in

a vowel (except **-ão**), add **s**: **os cafés, as bicas, os museus**.

a consonant (except **l** or **m**), add **-es**: **os portugueses, os elevadores, os rapazes**. Nouns ending in **s**, and not stressed on the final syllable, do not change in the plural (**o lápis — os lápis**).

The others are a little more complicated. Nouns ending in

-ão usually change to **-ões** (**as estações, as regiões**); a few change to **-ães** (**o cão — os cães, o pão — os pães**); some simply add **s** (**a mão — as mãos, o irmão — os irmãos**).

-al, -el, -il (if stressed) and **-ol**, change to **-ais, -éis, -is** and **-óis** (**o jornal — os jornais, o pastel — os pastéis, o barril — os barris, o lençol — os lençóis**).

-il (if unstressed), change to **-eis** (**o têxtil — os têxteis**).

-m, change to **-ns**: **o homem — os homens, o fim — os fins, o som — os sons, o atum — os atuns**).

6 Adjectives

6.1 Agreement

Adjectives (words that describe) agree in gender and number with the nouns they refer to, e.g.

um copo limpo	*a clean glass*
as toalhas limpas	*the clean towels*
o café e o açúcar brasileiros	*Brazilian coffee and sugar*
a casa e a rua vazias	*the empty house and street*

When the adjective refers to both a masculine and a feminine noun, the masculine plural is used, e.g.

o peixe e a carne grelhados   *the grilled fish and meat*

6.2 Gender (masculine / feminine)

Adjectives are given in dictionaries in the masculine singular form. In some cases there is no difference between masculine and feminine. Most adjectives, however, do have a feminine form, ending in **a**.

To form the feminine, adjectives ending in

-o: (except **-ão**) change to **-a**, e.g. **branco — branca**
-es: usually add **-a**, e.g. **português — portuguesa**
-or: usually add **-a**, e.g. **falador — faladora** *(talkative);* some very
   common adjectives with this ending are invariable: **melhor, pior,**
   maior, menor.
-u: add **-a**, e.g. **cru — crua** *(raw),* **nu — nua** *(naked)*
-eu: change to **-eia**, e.g. **europeu — europeia**
-ão: change to **-ona**, e.g. **brincalhão — brincalhona** *(playful);* or to **-ã**,
   e.g. **alemão — alemã.**

Most adjectives with endings other than the above have the same form in both the masculine and the feminine.

Two common exceptions are **bom — boa**, and **mau — má**.

6.3 Plurals

To form the plural, singular adjectives work in the same way as nouns (see 5.2 above).

6.4 Position

An adjective most frequently follows the noun to which it refers. However, the position can vary. Adjectives which normally follow the noun have their literal or objective meaning in this position; when placed before the noun they may express an emotional quality or a subjective judgement, e.g.

um homem grande   *a large man*
um grande homem   *a great man*
uma casa velha   *an old house* (simply a statement about its age)
Somos velhos amigos   *We're old friends* (a statement about the length
   and quality of the friendship)

Common adjectives which normally come before the noun are **bom** and **mau**, unless themselves qualified in some way, e.g.

um bom filme
um filme muito bom

6.5 *More / less, most / least*

You can qualify adjectives by using **mais**, **menos**, **bastante** etc. in front, e.g.

mais barato	*cheaper / cheapest*
menos caro	*less / least expensive*
mais pequeno	*smaller / smallest*

In a few cases, however, a different word is required to convey the idea of *more…*: **maior** *(larger)*, **melhor** *(better)*, **pior** *(worse)*.

6.6 *Very and too*

Portuguese uses **muito** for both *very* and *too*. In cases where there is a distinction in English, in Portuguese the meaning will often be clear from the context, e.g.

Este café é muito bom	*This coffee is very good*
As calças são muito grandes	*The trousers are very / too big*

Portuguese also forms superlatives by adding **-íssimo** to the last consonant of the adjective. The stress shifts to the first syllable of **-íssimo**.

Esta pensão é barata	*This guest-house is cheap*
Esta pensão é baratíssima	*This guest-house is very cheap*

In some cases (e.g. adjectives ending in **-co** or **-ca**), the spelling changes slightly in the superlative, to convey the sound in the original ending of the adjective:

Ela é uma pessoa simpática	*She's a nice person*
Ela é uma pessoa simpatiquíssima	*She's an extremely nice person*

In a few cases the superlatives are irregular:

Este vinho é mau	*This wine is bad*
Este vinho é péssimo!	*This wine is awful!*
Está bom?	*Are you well?*
Óptimo!	*Splendid!*

7 Pronouns

7.1 Subject pronouns (*I, she, it,* etc.)

In the following list the verb **falar** is used to show which verb form corresponds to each subject pronoun.

singular	*1st person*	eu	falo	*I speak*
	2nd person	tu	falas	*you speak*
	3rd person	você o senhor a senhora ele, ela	fala	*you* ⎫ *you* ⎬ *speak* *you* ⎭ *he / she speaks*
plural	*1st person*	nós	falamos	*we speak*
	2nd person	vós	falais	*you speak*
	3rd person	vocês os senhores as senhoras eles, elas	falam	*you* ⎫ *you* ⎬ *speak* *you* ⎭ *they speak*

The plural of **tu** is NOT **vós**, but **vocês** (with the 3rd person plural form of the verb). That is, **vocês** serves as the plural of both **você** and **tu**.

The second person plural **vós** has a restricted use (e.g. in the language of religious ceremonies, and sometimes in public speeches). It is useful to be able to recognise it when you come across it, but you will not need to use it.

The various words for *you* imply different degrees of formality. See Unit 2, section 3.

The subject pronouns are not normally used with verbs, since the verb ending indicates the subject. However, the subject pronoun is often necessary in order to avoid ambiguity, or to give emphasis where in English speech you would stress the pronoun.

Prefiro ir hoje   *I prefer to go today*
Você quer ir amanhã mas *You want to go tomorrow but I*
 eu prefiro ir hoje   *prefer to go today*

7.2 Object pronouns (*me, him, it* etc.)

The forms and use of object pronouns in Portuguese are complex and are only touched on briefly in this course (see Unit 5, sections 20, 21 and 24).

The following is not a complete explanation, but is intended as a guide to help you recognise pronouns when you come across them in the spoken or written language.

The object pronouns (with the subject pronouns to which they correspond) are:

	Subject	Direct object	Indirect object
1st person	eu	me	me
2nd person	tu	te	te
3rd person	você etc. ele ela	o, a o a	lhe
1st person	nós	nos	nos
2nd person	vós	vos	vos
3rd person	vocês etc. eles elas	os, as os as	lhes

Examples of direct object:

Conheço-o   *I know you / him / it*
Vi-a ontem   *I saw you / her / it yesterday*
Convido-as   *I invite you / them* (women)
Vejo-os amanhã   *I'll see them tomorrow* (men or things)

Examples of indirect object:

Deu-lhes o recado   *He gave them the message*
Fizeram-me um grande favor   *They have done me a great favour*
Escrevo-lhes todos os dias   *I write to them every day*
Entreguei-lhe o dinheiro   *I handed over the money to him / her*

7.3 After a preposition the pronouns required are identical to the subject pronouns, except for **mim** (in place of **me**) and **ti** (in place of **te**), e.g.

Para mim, uma cerveja *For me, a beer*
Falo com eles amanhã   *I'll talk to them tomorrow*

With the preposition **com**, however, the contracted forms **comigo**, **contigo**, **connosco** and **convosco** are used.

Quer falar comigo? *Do you want to talk to me?*
Vem connosco?   *Are you coming with us?*

7.4 Reflexives (*myself* etc.)

These refer back to the subject of the verb, and are used with verbs that are followed by **-se**, e.g. **chamar-se** *(to be called)*, **levantar-se** *(to get up)*.

	Subject pronoun	Reflexive pronoun
1st person	eu	me
2nd person	tu	te
3rd person	você, etc. ele ela	se
1st person	nós	nos
2nd person	vós	vos
3rd person	vocês eles elas	se

Chamo-me João   *My name is John*
Levantam-se cedo   *They get up early*
Este vinho serve-se fresco   *This wine is served cool*

7.5 Position

Object pronouns sometimes follow the verb, and sometimes come before it.

When they follow the verb, they are linked to it by a hyphen.

The easiest guide is to think of the object pronoun as normally following the verb. There are then a number of exceptions.

They precede the verb

in negative statements:

Não se chama Pedro   *His name isn't Peter*
Esse trabalho? Não o faço hoje   *That work? I'll not do it today*

after interrogative words (*who?, what?* etc.):

Como se chama?   *What's your name?*
Quem a viu?   *Who saw her?*

after relatives (*that, which, who* etc.):

A pessoa que o viu...   *The person who saw him...*
O empregado que nos serviu...   *The waiter who served us...*

after a few other individual words (e.g. **já, todo, também**):

Já me disse   *He has already told me*
Todos a admiram   *They all admire her*

7.6 Contraction

Contraction involving pronouns occurs in a number of situations. One of the most common is when **o, a, os** or **as** follows a verb form ending in **r** (e.g. the infinitive) or **s** (e.g. the *we* form).

Gosto desta blusa. Posso prová-la? (provar + a)	*I like this blouse. Can I try it on?*
Esse trabalho? Vou fazê-lo hoje (fazer + o)	*That work? I'm going to do it today*
Vamos abri-lo? (abrir + o)	*Are we going to open it?*
Compramo-los aqui? (compramos + os)	*Shall we buy them here?*

8 Relative pronouns

Que *(who, whom, which, that)* is by far the most common.

a pessoa que veio ontem	*the person who came yesterday*
o jornal que estou a ler	*the paper (that) I'm reading*
o hotel em que estamos	*the hotel (that) we're in*
o homem que vi na praia	*the man (that/whom) I saw on the beach*

When there is no reference to a specific noun, **o que** is used:

O que deve fazer é...	*What you must do is...*
Ela chegou tarde, o que me surpreendeu	*She arrived late, which surprised me*

Quem is used after a preposition, when referring to people:

a pessoa com quem falei	*the person (that) I spoke to*

9 Verbs

9.1

There are three types of verb: one with the infinitive ending in **-ar**, one ending in **-er** and one ending in **-ir**.

9.2 Regular verbs

Regular verbs of all three types follow the pattern of the examples below. For each verb the table gives: the infinitive; the past participle; one form of the present subjunctive (used in giving commands and instructions); and all the forms for three tenses – present, imperfect and preterite. The four most useful forms for the beginner are the four corresponding to:

eu
ele, ela, você, o senhor, a senhora
nós
eles, elas, vocês, os senhores, as senhoras

The **vós** form has a restricted use in modern Portuguese. It occurs in the language of religious ceremonies and, often, of public speeches. You may want to be able to recognise it, but you will not need to use it.

Infinitive	falar	comer	partir
Past participle	falado	comido	partido
Present subjunctive	fale	coma	parta
Present eu tu ele, ela, você, etc. nós vós eles, elas, vocês, etc.	falo falas fala falamos falais falam	como comes come comemos comeis comem	parto partes parte partimos partis partem
Imperfect eu tu ele, ela, você, etc. nós vós eles, elas, vocês, etc.	falava falavas falava falávamos faláveis falavam	comia comias comia comíamos comíeis comiam	partia partias partia partíamos partíeis partiam
Preterite eu tu ele, ela, você, etc. nós vós eles, elas, vocês, etc.	falei falaste falou falámos falastes falaram	comi comeste comeu comemos comestes comeram	parti partiste partiu partimos partistes partiram

9.3 Irregular verbs

There are also a number of irregular verbs in common use, which vary from the above patterns to a greater or lesser extent. Some of the most frequently used are given below.

A number of other irregular verbs are included in the Glossary, with a brief indication of the irregularity. For these a reference grammar or dictionary should be consulted.

Infinitive	**dar**	**dizer**	**estar**	**fazer**
Past participle	dado	dito	estado	feito
Present subjunctive	dê	diga	esteja	faça
Present	dou dás dá damos dais dão	digo dizes diz dizemos dizeis dizem	estou estás está estamos estais estão	faço fazes faz fazemos fazeis fazem
Imperfect	dava, etc. *(regular)*	dizia, etc. *(regular)*	estava, etc. *(regular)*	fazia, etc. *(regular)*
Preterite	dei deste deu demos destes deram	disse disseste disse dissemos dissestes disseram	estive estiveste esteve estivemos estivestes estiveram	fiz fizeste fez fizemos fizestes fizeram

Infinitive	**pôr**	**querer**	**saber**	**ser**
Past participle	posto	querido	sabido	sido
Present subjunctive	ponha	queira	saiba	seja
Present	ponho pões põe pomos pondes põem	quero queres quer queremos quereis querem	sei sabes sabe sabemos sabeis sabem	sou és é somos sois são
Imperfect	punha punhas punha púnhamos púnheis punham	queria, etc. *(regular)*	sabia, etc. *(regular)*	era eras era éramos éreis eram
Preterite	pus puseste pôs pusemos pusestes puseram	quis quiseste quis quisemos quisestes quiseram	soube soubeste soube soubemos soubestes souberam	fui foste foi fomos fostes foram

Infinitive	haver	ir	ler	poder
Past participle	havido	ido	lido	podido
Present subjunctive	haja	vá	leia	possa
Present	hei hás há havemos haveis hão	vou vais vai vamos ides vão	leio lês lê lemos ledes lêem	posso podes pode podemos podeis podem
Imperfect	havia, etc. (regular)	ia, etc. (regular)	lia, etc. (regular)	podia, etc. (regular)
Preterite	houve houveste houve houvemos houvestes houveram	fui foste foi fomos fostes foram	li (regular)	pude pudeste pôde pudemos pudestes puderam

Infinitive	ter	trazer	ver	vir
Past participle	tido	trazido	visto	vindo
Present subjunctive	tenha	traga	veja	venha
Present	tenho tens tem temos tendes têm	trago trazes traz trazemos trazeis trazem	vejo vês vê vemos vedes vêem	venho vens vem vimos vindes vêm
Imperfect	tinha tinhas tinha tínhamos tínheis tinham	trazia, etc. (regular)	via, etc. (regular)	vinha vinhas vinha vínhamos vínheis vinham
Preterite	tive tiveste teve tivemos tivestes tiveram	trouxe trouxeste trouxe trouxemos trouxestes trouxeram	vi viste viu vimos vistes viram	vim vieste veio viemos viestes vieram

9.4 The infinitive

This is the form in which verbs are given in dictionaries. Common uses are:

after another verb (or a verb + a preposition):

Queria almoçar	*I'd like to have lunch*
Tenho de ir ao banco	*I have to go to the bank*
Preciso de comprar pão	*I need to buy bread*

after words for *before, after* etc.:

Antes de partir,...	*Before leaving,...*
Ao chegar,...	*On arriving,...*
Depois de jantar,...	*After having dinner,...*

in instructions or prohibitions:

Consumir até Julho de 1987	*Use before July 1987*
Não fumar	*No smoking*
Não tocar	*Do not touch*

when the verb is used as a noun:

Deitar cedo e cedo erguer	*Early to bed and early to rise*
Dá saúde e faz crescer	*Makes a man healthy, wealthy and wise*
(proverb)	(literally ...*gives you health and makes you grow*)

9.5 The present tense

Most uses of the present tense are similar to English. It is used to refer to something that is the case at the time of speaking:

Trabalha numa fábrica	*He works in a factory*
Falam português	*They speak Portuguese*
Não gosto de chá	*I don't like tea*

As in English, its uses include:

what normally / occasionally happens or is the case:

Leio o jornal todos os dias	*I read the paper every day*
Em Agosto faz muito calor	*In August it's very hot*
Às vezes vamos de táxi	*Sometimes we go by taxi*

what is intended or will happen in the future (when this future is shown elsewhere in the sentence):

Chega a Lisboa amanhã	*He arrives (he's arriving) in Lisbon tomorrow*
Ficamos até sábado	*We'll be staying until Saturday*
Telefono hoje à noite	*I'll phone tonight*

what has happened in the past (when telling a story, or in historical narrative):

Em 1500 Cabral descobre o Brasil	*In 1500 Cabral discovers Brazil*
A 25 de Abril o regime de Caetano rende-se	*On the 25th of April the Caetano regime surrenders*

NB If the emphasis is on what is happening at the moment (English *I am… — ing*) Portuguese uses the present of **estar** (+ **a**):

Está a trabalhar numa fábrica	*He is working in a factory*
Estou a ler um romance	*I'm reading a novel*
Estamos a chegar	*We're just arriving* (i.e. *just about to arrive*)

Unlike English, the present is also used to talk about what has been happening until now and is still going on. This use involves **desde** or constructions with **há**:

Desde Janeiro de 1986 Portugal **é membro da CEE**	*Since January 1986 Portugal has* *been a member of the EEC*
Estou aqui há um mês	*I've been here for a month*
Vamos a este café desde há anos	*We've been going to this café for years*

9.6 The imperfect

This is used in describing past states and to talk about what used to happen, or was happening at some time in the past.

Antigamente, Lisboa era **uma cidade mais tranquila**	*Formerly, Lisbon was a* *quieter city*
Morávamos naquela casa	*We lived (used to live) in that house*
Ia à praia aos sábados	*I went (used to go) to the beach* *on Saturdays*

The imperfect is also commonly used where English uses *would*:

Queria um café	*I'd like a coffee*
Era boa ideia	*It would be a good idea*
Não sei se tinha tempo	*I don't know if I would have time*

9.7 The preterite

This is used to tell of past events:

Tomei o pequeno almoço às 8.00	*I had breakfast at 8.00*
Voltaram a Portugal em 1974	*They returned to Portugal in 1974*
Ontem fomos ao teatro	*Yesterday we went to the theatre*

English-speakers often have some difficulty knowing whether to use the imperfect or the preterite in Portuguese, where the English is *I did, I…ed*. This question is dealt with in the Anthology, text 7, note 1.

A major difference from English is that the preterite is also used where English uses *I have done*. In this use, the preterite sometimes follows **já**:

Já acabou?	*Have you finished?*
Trabalhámos muito	*We have worked hard*
Almoçaram?	*Have you had lunch?*

9.8 The past participle

As in English, the past participle can be used as an adjective:

batatas cozidas	*boiled potatoes*
truta grelhada	*grilled trout*
lulas fritas	*fried squid*

It can be used with **ser** as a way of forming the passive. In this case, like an adjective, it agrees in number and gender with what it refers to.

Fui convidada *I was invited* (a woman speaking)
O discurso foi lido *The speech was read*
Fomos apanhados *We were caught*

It is also used to form the compound perfect tense (see below).

9.9 The compound perfect

This consists of the appropriate form of **ter** (occasionally, in written language, **haver**), combined with the past participle.

Its use is restricted to talking about what has been happening regularly, since some time in the past up to now. It is often the equivalent of the English *have been … ing.*

Temos visto muitos filmes *We've been seeing a lot of films*
Têm vindo todos os dias *They have been coming every day*
Tenho estado doente *I've been ill (and am still not better)*

For the equivalent of the English *have done,* see 9.7.

9.10 The present subjunctive

Only one form of the present subjunctive is given in the verb table earlier: the first person *(I)*, which in fact is identical to the third person *(he / she / you).* With a few exceptions, this form of the present subjunctive of any verb can be found by taking the *I* form of the present tense and changing the final vowel. If the infinitive of the verb ends in **-ar**, the final vowel of the present subjunctive is **e**. If the infinitive ends in **-er** or **-ir**, the final vowel of the present subjunctive is **a**, e.g.

Infinitive		*Present*	*Present subjunctive*
falar	(eu)	**falo**	**fale**
comprar		compro	compre
beber		bebo	beba
fazer		faço	faça
seguir		sigo	siga
vir		venho	venha

9.11 Uses

The third person of the present subjunctive is used as a way of giving directions and instructions:

Siga em frente *Carry on straight ahead*
Vire à sua direita *Turn to your right*
Empurre *Push*
Puxe *Pull*

See also Unit 4, section 15.

NOTE: The rest of Section 9 deals briefly with a few aspects which lie beyond the scope of the course. The following paragraphs are intended as an aid to a fuller understanding of the materials in the Anthology.

9.12 Other uses of the subjunctive

A common use is after verbs of wanting, hoping, doubting and requesting:

Quer que venhamos logo? *Do you want us to come immediately?*
Espero que não cheguem *I hope they won't arrive*
 muito tarde *very late*
Duvido que o possa fazer hoje *I doubt whether I can do it today*

9.13 The 'personal' infinitive

In certain situations in Portuguese, the infinitive is used with an ending that indicates a subject (the person or thing doing the action in question). Being able to use this personal infinitive with ease is quite an advanced skill, and it is not essential in the early stages of learning Portuguese.

However, it will help you to understand both the spoken and the written language if you can recognise this form of the infinitive, and distinguish it from another verb form which has identical endings — the future subjunctive.

The endings are **-es** (indicating that the subject is **tu**), **-mos** (indicating **nós**), **-des** (**vós**) and **-em** (**eles, vocês** etc.).

To form the personal infinitive, these endings are added to the infinitive.

To arrive at the future subjunctive, you start from the *they* form of the preterite, drop the **-am** ending, and substitute the new ending.

In the case of **fazer**, for example, this gives:

	Inflected infinitive	*Future subjunctive*
eu	fazer	fizer
tu	fazeres	fizeres
ele, você, etc.	fazer	fizer
nós	fazermos	fizermos
vós	fazerdes	fizerdes
eles, vocês, etc.	fazerem	fizerem

9.14 Uses of the personal infinitive

Among the various uses of the personal infinitive, a common one is when the subject of the main verb is different from that of the infinitive:

É melhor irmos hoje *It's best to go (i.e. it's best if we go) today*
Antes de almoçarmos, *Before having lunch (i.e. before we have*
 tenho de ir ao banco *lunch), I need to go to the bank*
Dou-lhes o recado logo *I'll give them the message as*
 depois de eles chegarem *soon as they arrive*

9.15 Uses of the future subjunctive

You will find the future subjunctive used after **se** *(if)*, **quando**, and relative pronouns (e.g. **que**), when the phrase refers to the future:

Se tiver tempo, falo com ela amanhã	*If I have time, I'll talk to her tomorrow*
Quando chegarmos à praça, o café é à nossa direita	*When we reach the square, the café is on our right*
Os que quiserem podem ficar	*Those who wish may stay*

10 Adverbs

10.1 The most common adverbs relate to

time: **ontem, hoje, amanhã, agora**, etc.
place: **aqui, ali, perto, longe**, etc.
manner: **bem, melhor, mal, pior**, etc.
quantity: **muito, pouco, nada, mais, menos, bastante**, etc.

10.2 Just as you can form an adverb in English by adding *-ly* to the adjective, in Portuguese adverbs can be formed from most adjectives by adding **-mente** to the feminine form, e.g. **completo — completamente, inteiro — inteiramente, necessário — necessariamente.**

In some cases, of course, there is no difference between masculine and feminine in the adjective. In such cases you simply add **-mente** to the adjective: **feliz — felizmente, simples — simplesmente.**

11 Interrogatives

11.1 Questions which can be answered by *yes, no, perhaps,* etc. may be formulated in Portuguese in exactly the same way as a statement, with no alteration in word order. In speech, the query is indicated by the tone of voice (see Unit 1, sections 17 and 18), e.g. **O senhor fala português? Vocês gostam do café?**

11.2 For other types of question, the common interrogative words in Portuguese are given below. In these kinds of question, if the subject of the verb is stated it normally follows the verb.

Quem? *Who?*	
Quem fala?	*Who is speaking?*
Quem é o senhor?	*Who are you?*

De quem? *Whose?*	
De quem é este jornal?	*Whose is this newspaper?*

Onde? (stationary) *Where?*	
Onde é a Praça de Camões?	*Where is the Praça de Camões?*

Aonde? (=a+onde)	} *Where (to)?*
Para onde?	
Aonde foram?	*Where did they go?*
Para onde vai?	*Where are you going?*

Donde? (=de + onde)   *Where (from)?*
O senhor, donde é?   *Where are you from?*

Como?   *How?*
Como está o filho dela?   *How is her son?*
Como se chama a senhora?   *What is your name?*

Porquê?   *Why?*
Porque diz isso?   *Why do you say that?*

(When it stands on its own, as the question *Why?*, **Porquê?** is stressed on the final syllable, and is written with an accent on the **e**. In all other situations, **porque** is stressed on the first syllable.)

Quanto(s) -a(s)?   *How much? How many?*
Quanto é?   *How much is it?*
Quantos são?   *How many are you?*

A como é...?   *How much...?*
A como é o presunto?   *How much is the ham?*
A como são as maçãs?   *How much are the apples?*

(The use of **a como é...?** is restricted to asking prices of goods sold by weight — see Unit 5, section 13.)

The following are a bit more complicated. **Que...?**, unless followed immediately by a noun, is usually interchangeable with **o que...?**

Que?   *What? Which?*
Que marca prefere?   *Which / What make do you prefer?*
Que horas são?   *What time is it?*

O que?   *What?*
O que estão a fazer?   *What are they doing?*

Qual? Quais?   *Which? What?*
Qual é a melhor estrada?   *Which is the best road?*
Qual é a sua morada?   *What is your address?*
Quais recomenda?   *Which ones do you recommend?*

(On **Qual é...?**, see Unit 3, section 3.)

11.3   A very common construction in questions is to insert **é que** after the interrogative word:

O que é que está a fazer?   *What are you doing?*
Como é que se chama?   *What's your name?*
Porque é que diz isso?   *Why do you say that?*

12 Numbers

12.1 Numbers from zero to nine hundred:

0 zero	10 dez		
1 um / uma	11 onze	10 dez	100 cem
2 dois / duas	12 doze	20 vinte	200 duzentos, -as
3 três	13 treze	30 trinta	300 trezentos, -as
4 quatro	14 catorze	40 quarenta	400 quatrocentos, -as
5 cinco	15 quinze	50 cinquenta	500 quinhentos, -as
6 seis	16 dezasseis	60 sessenta	600 seiscentos, -as
7 sete	17 dezassete	70 setenta	700 setecentos, -as
8 oito	18 dezoito	80 oitenta	800 oitocentos, -as
9 nove	19 dezanove	90 noventa	900 novecentos, -as

12.2 From 21 to 29, 31 to 39, etc.:

21 vinte e um / uma	31 trinta e um / uma
22 vinte e dois / duas	32 trinta e dois / duas
23 vinte e três	33 trinta e três
etc.	etc.

12.3 From 101 to 119:   From 120 to 199:

101 cento e um / uma	120 cento e vinte
102 cento e dois / duas	121 cento e vinte e um / uma
103 cento e três	122 cento e vinte e dois / duas
etc.	123 cento e vinte e três
	etc.

12.4 From 200 to 299, 300 to 399, etc.:

201 duzentos (-as) e um (uma)
202 duzentos (-as) e dois (duas)
203 duzentos (-as) e três
    etc.

12.5 Thousands

1000 mil
2000 dois / duas mil
3000 três mil
100 000 cem mil
200 000 duzentos (-as) mil
300 000 trezentos (-as) mil
    etc.

From 1001 to 1100, 2001 to 2100, etc., **mil** is followed by **e**:

1001 mil e um / uma
1066 mil e sessenta e seis
2100 dois mil e cem

When **mil** is followed by hundreds **e** is used after **mil** only if the number ends -00:

1100 mil e cem
4200 quatro mil e duzentos (-as)
But:
1755 mil setecentos e cinquenta e cinco
1974 mil novecentos e setenta e quatro

12.6   Millions

1 000 000 um milhão (de)
2 000 000 dois milhões (de)

Numbers between one and two million are the only ones where **um** is used before the number, e.g. **um milhão e oitocentas mil pessoas** (one million eight hundred thousand people).

Portuguese differs in this respect from English, where we also say *a/one hundred...* and *a/one thousand...*

When expressing round figures (**um milhão, dois milhões** etc.) **de** is used as a link if a noun follows, e.g.: **um milhão de contos** *a million* **contos** (i.e. a billion **escudos**), **dois milhões de habitantes** *two million inhabitants.* However, when expressing figures in between round millions, **de** is omitted, e.g.: **três milhões e quinhentos mil habitantes**.

12.7   Agreement

The words for numbers do not change, except for **um (uma)**, **dois (duas)** and the hundreds from **duzentos (-as)** to **novecentos (-as)**, which agree in gender with the noun:

um café	**uma cerveja**
dois garotos	**duas bicas**
duzentos e vinte e um homens	**duzentas e vinte e uma pessoas**

12.8   Ordinal numbers (*first, second,* etc.)

1st primeiro, -a	6th sexto, -a
2nd segundo, -a	7th sétimo, -a
3rd terceiro, -a	8th oitavo, -a
4th quarto, -a	9th nono, -a
5th quinto, -a	10th décimo, -a

The ordinals beyond **décimo** are less commonly used.

KEY TO EXERCISES

The numbers in the margin refer to the sections of each unit. Optional words are in brackets, e.g. **Como (é que) se chama?** means you can say either **Como é que se chama?** or **Como se chama?** Alternative forms are separated by / (e.g. **é / fica**). Where either a masculine or feminine ending is possible, this is also indicated by /, e.g. **obrigado / a** (**obrigado** if you are a man, **obrigada** if you are a woman).

Unit 1

4. Bárbara says: 'Sou de Dublim'; Vítor: 'Sou de Edimburgo'; Sónia: 'Sou de Londres'.

9. Carlos.

10. Helena.

12. Starting from **uma água mineral sem gás**, the numbers should read: 7, 6, 4, 1, 10, 8, 3, 2 and 9, 5, 11.

13. Uma bica, um garoto, um chá com leite e um chá de limão, se faz favor; Mais nada, obrigado / a; Quanto é?

14. The waiter misses out **um chá**. He is right in saying **um chá de limão** but gets the number wrong with all the other items.

19. John é de Londres. Fala inglês; Maria é de Dublim. Fala inglês e português; Marta é de Lisboa. Fala português; Sónia é de São Paulo. Fala inglês e português; Pedro é de Lisboa. Fala português.

Mais alguma coisa?

1. dia; se; me; de; escocês.

2. Que; Uma; um; de; com; alguma; mineral; natural; favor; é.

3. 1 pastel   2 chá   3 sem   4 leite   5 fresco   6 inglês   7 água
8 obrigado / a   9 mais   10 nada   11 pastelaria.

Unit 2

4. 1. Bom dia; (Estou) bem, obrigado / a. E a senhora?
   2. Boa noite; (Estou) bem, obrigado / a. E o senhor?

5. Faz favor, tem… 1 chá?   2 manteiga?   3 fiambre?   4 café?

8. 1 três   2 cinco   3 quatro   4 seis.

9. (Estou) bem, obrigado / a. E o senhor?; Tem uma mesa para duas pessoas?; Está bem, obrigado / a; Duas cervejas e duas sanduíches de fiambre, se faz favor.

11. Com licença; Desculpe!; Boa noite. Tem uma mesa?; Não, somos seis; Está bem, obrigado / a; Com licença. Posso?

16. Faz favor!; Queríamos dois copos de vinho tinto; Tem rissóis?; Queria quatro, se faz favor.

17. Queria um chá sem leite e um garoto, se faz favor; Faz favor!; Desculpe. Queria também dois pastéis de nata; Mais nada, obrigado / a.

21. Items chosen are (in this order): frango piri-piri; rissóis de camarão; espetada mista; bacalhau assado; caldo verde; omeleta de presunto; uma garrafa de vinho branco.

22. Items chosen are (in this order): mousse de chocolate; queijo da serra; bolo de amêndoa; uma maçã.

Mais alguma coisa?

1 Como 2 Estou 3 pessoas 4 temos 5 lista 6 certeza 7 arroz
8 porco 9 dose 10 também 11 beber 12 garrafa 13 sem
14 natural 15 nada.

Unit 3

2. Gosto de… / Não gosto de… 1 cerveja 2 queijo 3 vinho
4 peixe.

4. 1 Este é o meu comboio 2 Esta é a minha mala 3 Este é o meu autocarro 4 Este é o meu bilhete.

6. 1 no 2 de; na 3 do 4 de 5 à; do 6 da 7 no; da.

8. 1 de autocarro 2 de comboio 3 a pé 4 de carro.

14. You're in Lisbon, in a hotel in the Avenida da República. You want to visit Sintra. The trains for Sintra leave from Rossio station. You call a taxi.

15. Para a estação do Rossio, se faz favor; Quanto é?; (Queria um bilhete) para Sintra, se faz favor; De ida e volta; Quanto é?

18. 1 É meio-dia e vinte / É meia-noite e vinte.
2 São seis menos dez / São cinco e cinquenta.
3 É uma e um quarto / É uma e quinze.
4 São nove e meia / São nove e trinta.
5 São quatro menos um quarto / São quatro menos quinze / São três e quarenta e cinco.
6 São oito e vinte e cinco.
7 São três menos cinco / São duas e cinquenta e cinco.
8 São duas e um quarto / São duas e quinze.
9 É meio-dia menos vinte / É meia-noite menos vinte / São onze e quarenta.
10 São cinco menos vinte e cinco / São quatro e trinta e cinco.
11 São onze e meia / São onze e trinta.
12 São nove e dez.

20. 1 Oporto 2 single 3 mil trezentos e oitenta escudos (1380$00)
    4 15.30 5 19.45 6 platform 3.

23. 1 Na quinta-feira 2 Na segunda-feira 3 Na quarta-feira
    4 No sábado 5 Na sexta-feira 6 Na terça-feira.

24. Segunda, quarta e quinta-feira: trezentos e sessenta escudos.
    Terça-feira: quatrocentos e quarenta escudos.
    Sexta-feira: trezentos e setenta escudos.
    Sábado: quatrocentos escudos.

Unit 4

2. 1 Há um restaurante aqui perto? 2 Há comboios para Sintra?
   3 Há um avião para Londres à uma e meia? 4 Há autocarros
   do aeroporto para o centro da cidade? 5 Há uma camioneta às seis
   e meia para Setúbal? 6 Há uma pensão aqui perto?
   7 Há eléctricos para Belém? 8 Há um café na praça?

4. 1 estão 2 está̃ 3 estou 4 estão 5 Estamos 6 está.

6. 1 Onde é / fica o Hotel Capitol?; É / Fica
   2 Há uma farmácia?; Há
   3 Onde estão os meus bilhetes?; Estão
   4 Onde é / fica o banco mais próximo?; É / Fica
   5 Onde está o nosso carro?; Está

7. 1 behind 2 on the left-hand side (of) 3 in the middle (of)
   4 at the far end (of) 5 on the right-hand side (of) 6 between
   7 beside.

8. Sim: 2, 3, 5, 6, 7, 10. Não: 1, 4, 8, 9, 11, 12.

12. A Rua dos Fanqueiros.

13. esquerda; fim; direita; frente.

14. Pedro's route takes him past the three sets of traffic lights. At the
    third set, he turns right and carries on. The bank is then on his left,
    at the street corner (top right on plan).

17. Jorge: one right turn, one left turn.
    Maria: right.

19. **vago** (vacant); **uma vaga** (a vacancy); **ocupado** (occupied).

20. At the end of the street.

21. **um quarto simples** (a single room); **um quarto duplo / um quarto
    de casal** (a double room).

22. Single room: 2800$00; double room: 3300$00.

23. **o banho** (the bath); **a casa de banho** (the bathroom).

24. To the right.

25. vagos; casal; casal; casa; preço; São; cinco; as; é / fica; andar; Há;
    Com; ao; pequeno; Obrigado / a.

3. 11.45; 1.00.

4. Faz favor, ainda há... 1 fruta? 2 carne? 3 peixe? 4 pão?

6. 1 Temos de ir à frutaria. 2 Tenho de ir à peixaria. 3 Tenho de ir ao talho. 4 Temos de ir à padaria. 5 Temos de ir à mercearia. 6 Tenho de ir à farmácia. 7 Temos de ir à pastelaria.

8. Trocar; cambiar.

9. 1 cento e quarenta e oito 2 cento e quarenta e nove 3 trezentos 4 cento e oitenta e sete.

10. Left.

11. 1 your passport 2 sign the cheque 3 your address 4 go to the cashier's desk.

Your part of the dialogue is:

Bom dia. Posso cambiar / trocar um cheque de cinquenta libras?
Tenho, sim.
Estou no Hotel Fénix, Praça Marquês de Pombal, 8.
Obrigado / a.

12. Starting from **No correio, que fica aqui na praça,** the **Respostas** should be numbered 7, 5, 6, 1, 2, 8, 4, 3.

14. Presunto: mil trezentos e catorze escudos; Chouriço: quinhentos e vinte e cinco escudos, mil cento e trinta escudos.

15. Beginning with **2 quilos de batatas,** the prices are: setenta e dois; quinhentos e sessenta e cinco; oitenta; cinquenta e quatro; cento e noventa e oito; setecentos e vinte; cento e sete; trezentos e cinquenta. Total: dois mil cento e quarenta e seis.

16. quilo; garrafas; litro; dúzia; pacote; frasco.

18. Desculpe, há uma mercearia aqui perto?; Obrigado / a; Boa tarde. (Queria) um quilo de arroz e meio quilo de café, se faz favor; Um pacote de manteiga e meio litro de azeite; Queria também uma caixa de marmelada e um quilo de açúcar; Mais nada, obrigado / a. Quanto é?; Tem troco de cinco contos / cinco mil escudos?; Obrigado / a.

22. 1 white 2 brown 3 blue 4 red 5 grey 6 grey.

23. Following the order of the questions on the cassette, your answers are: Gosto. Posso... prová-la, prová-la, prová-lo, prová-la, prová-lo, prová-lo.

25. Boa tarde. Queria ver uma camisola de lã, se faz favor.
Gosto da cinzenta. Posso prová-la?
Não me fica muito bem.
Sim, gosto desta. Fica-me bem. Quanto é?
Não é nada cara. Levo-a.

29. 1 I   2 E   3 J   4 G   5 F   6 B   7 C   8 A   9 D   10 H.

30. 1 mais caro do que   2 maior do que   3 melhor do que
    4 mais barato do que   5 mais pequeno do que   6 melhor do que
    7 mais barata do que   8 maior do que   9 mais caro do que
    10 mais pequena do que.

31. 1 (O presunto) é a mil duzentos e cinquenta escudos o quilo.
    2 (A blusa de seda) são doze contos.
    3 (As calças) são três mil e quinhentos escudos /
      (As calças) são três contos e quinhentos.
    4 (O chouriço) é a quinhentos e oitenta escudos o quilo.
    5 (O café) é a dois mil e cem escudos o quilo.
    6 (O arroz) é a cento e sessenta e seis escudos o quilo.
    7 (O casaco) são oito contos.

Unit 6

2. Dialogue with porter:

   Boa tarde. Está avariado.
   Não, obrigado/a. Vou apanhar o autocarro.

   Dialogue with receptionist:

   Desculpe. O elevador não funciona?
   Mas o meu quarto é no sexto andar!
   Posso, sim… O meu carro também está avariado.

5. Estou.
   Fala o João Gomes.
   O meu frigorífico está avariado e queria falar com o Sr. Martins.
   Quando (é que) posso falar com ele?

8. (Daqui) fala o João Gomes. O Sr. Martins já está?
   Quando (é que) posso falar com ele?
   Está bem. Volto a telefonar hoje à tarde.
   Até logo.

Mais alguma coisa?

1. Bom dia. Preciso de fazer uma chamada.
   Seis nove, zero zero, cinco oito.
   Obrigada.
   Bom dia. Queria falar com o Sr. Sousa Matos.
   Volto a telefonar daqui a pouco.

2. Posso falar com o Sr. Sousa Matos?
   Fala Maria Fox.
   Estou bem, obrigada. E o senhor?
   Pode ser amanhã de manhã?
   Está bem. Então, até amanhã.

3. Bom dia. Sou Maria Fox. Tenho um encontro marcado com o
   Sr. Sousa Matos para as onze e um quarto.
   Obrigada.
   Onde é / fica a casa de banho?
   Só alguns minutos.
   Não faz mal / Não tem importância.

4. Vamos almoçar, então? Há um restaurante aqui perto?
   Fica longe? Podemos ir a pé?
   É, sim. Tem uma mesa para duas pessoas?
   Prefiro esta mesa aqui.
   Qual é o prato do dia?
   Queria a lista, se faz favor.

5. Queria o prato do dia / o bacalhau à Gomes de Sá, se faz favor.
   Uma garrafa do vinho tinto da casa.
   Faz favor!
   Duas bicas, e a conta, se faz favor.
   Posso levar o meu colega?
   Onde é que mora?
   A que horas começa a festa?
   Então, adeus. Até amanhã.

6. Boa tarde.
   Para a estação do Cais do Sodré, se faz favor.
   Quanto é?
   Tem troco dum conto / de mil escudos?
   Obrigada.
   Dois bilhetes de ida e volta para a Parede, se faz favor.
   A que horas parte o comboio?
   Qual é a linha?
   Obrigada.

7. Desculpe. (Podia-me dizer) onde (é que) fica / é a Rua Dr. João
   de Menezes, se faz favor?
   Fica longe?
   Obrigada.

   Queria apresentar o Sr. Brown.
   Não, só fala inglês.
   Sim, prefiro um sumo de laranja.
   Um whisky com água, se faz favor.
   Que horas são?
   Temos de voltar para Lisboa. O nosso voo é às dez e meia da
   manhã.
   Muito obrigada. Adeus. Até à próxima.

Glossary

A

a *the; her, it (pronoun)*
aberto *open*
Abril *April*
abrir *(pp.* aberto*) to open*
acabar *to finish*
achar *to find;* achar que *to think that*
o açúcar *sugar*
adeus *goodbye*
o aeroporto *airport*
afinal *at last; as it turns / turned out, actually*
a agência *agency*
Agosto *August*
agradável *pleasant, agreeable*
agrícola *agricultural*
a água *water;* água mineral *mineral water*
aí *there*
ainda *still;* ainda há…? *is / are there still…?*
a ajuda *help*
o álcool *alcohol*
além de *beyond*
alemão, alemã *German*
o algodão *cotton*
alguém *someone*

o alho *garlic*
ali *there, over there*
almoçar *to have lunch*
o almoço *lunch*
alugar *to rent, hire*
amanhã *tomorrow;* amanhã de manhã *tomorrow morning*
amarelo / a *yellow*
a amêijoa *clam, cockle*
a amêndoa *almond*
o amigo, a amiga *friend*
o ananás *pineapple*
o andar *floor;* o segundo andar *the second floor*
angolano / a *Angolan*
o animal *animal*
o ano *year*
antes (de) *before*
antigo / a *ancient, old; former*
apanhar *to catch; pick*
apertado / a *tight*
apontar *to note down*
apresentar *to introduce (someone)*
aquele, aquela *that, that one*
aqui *here*

aquilo *that*

arranja-me...? *have you got...? could you find me...?*

arranjar *to arrange; to manage to obtain*

o arroz *rice*

o artesanato *craft-work*

o artigo *article*

a aspirina *aspirin*

assado / a *roasted*

assim *so, thus, this way;* assim, assim *so so*

assinar *to sign*

até a *until*

o atractivo *attraction*

atrás (de) *behind*

atrasar-se *to be late*

atravessar *to cross*

o atum *tunny fish*

a aula *class*

o autocarro *bus*

avariado *out of order, broken down*

avariar-se *to go wrong, break down*

a avenida *avenue*

o avião *aeroplane*

o azar *bad luck*

o azeite *olive oil*

azul (*regular pl.* azuis) *blue*

B

o bacalhau *cod*

o bairro *district, quarter*

a baixa *city centre*

baixo / a *low;* em baixo *down below*

o balcão *counter (e.g. of a bank); bar (of a café)*

o banco *bank*

o banho *bath;* a casa de banho *bathroom*

o bar *bar*

barato / a *cheap*

o barco *boat*

o barril *barrel*

bastante *enough, quite*

a batata *potato*

beber *to drink*

a bebida *drink*

o beco *alley*

bem *well*

a bica *small, very strong black coffee*

a bicha *queue*

o bife *steak*

---

o bilhete *ticket*

a blusa *blouse*

um bocado *a little, a bit*

o bolo *cake, bun*

bom, boa (bons, boas) *good;* bom dia *good morning;* boa tarde *good afternoon;* boa noite *good evening, good night*

bonito / a *pretty*

bordado / a *embroidered*

o bordado *embroidery*

branco / a *white*

brasileiro / a *Brazilian*

C

a cabine *telephone booth*

o café *coffee, café*

a caixa *box; cash desk, till, check-out point*

a calçada *paved (originally cobbled) road*

as calças (*pl*) *trousers*

a caldeirada *fish stew*

o caldo *clear soup, broth*

o camarão *shrimp*

cambiar *to change*

o caminho *way, path;* o caminho de ferro *railway*

a camioneta *coach*

a camisola *pullover*

o cão (cães) *dog*

o carioca *weak black coffee*

a carne *meat*

caro / a *expensive, dear*

o carro *car*

o cartão *card; identity card, bank card, etc.*

a casa *house;* casa de banho *bathroom*

o casaco *jacket*

o casal *married couple;* um quarto de casal *a double room*

caseiro / a *home made*

castanho / a *brown*

a cebola *onion*

o centavo *one hundredth of an* escudo

o centro *centre*

a cerâmica *pottery, ceramics*

a certeza *certainty;* com certeza *certainly, of course;* de certeza *surely, definitely*

a cerveja *beer*

a cervejaria *alehouse (usually found as part of the name of a bar or restaurant where beer is a speciality)*

o cesto *basket*

o chá *tea*

a chamada *telephone call;* fazer uma
   chamada *to make a telephone call*
   chamar *to call*
   chamar-se *to be called;* chamo-me… *my
   name is…*

a chapa *metal disc (to mark your place in bank
   queues)*

a charcutaria *delicatessen, cold meats shop*

a chave *key*

o chefe *chef*

a chegada *arrival*
   chegar *to arrive;* chega *that's enough*

o cheque *cheque*

o chocolate *chocolate*

o chouriço *spicy sausage*

a cidade *city*

o cinema *cinema*
   cinzento/a *grey*

a coisa *thing*
   coitado/a *poor, wretched;* Coitado/a!
   Poor thing!

o/a colega *colleague*
   com *with*
   combinar *to fix, arrange (a time, place);* fica
   combinado para… *it's arranged for…*

o comboio *train*
   comer *to eat*
   como *as;* como? *how?;* como está? *how
   are you?;* a como é/são…? *how much
   is/are…?*

a compra *purchase;* fazer compras *to shop;*
   ir às compras *go shopping*
   comprar *to buy*
   consultar *to consult*

a conta *bill, account*
   continuar *to continue, go on*
um conto *a thousand* escudos

o copo *glass*

a cor *colour*

o corredor *corridor*

o correio *post office; mail*

a costeleta *chop*
   costumar *to be in the habit of;* costumo ir a
   pé *I usually walk*

a cotação *exchange rate*

o cozido *stew*
   cozido/a *boiled, baked*

190 o cruzamento *crossing*

a cultura *culture*
cultural *cultural*
custar *to cost;* quanto custa…? *how much
   does it cost?;* custa-me *it's difficult for me*

D

daqui *from here;* daqui a uma semana/
   a três dias *in a week/three days (from now)*
dar *(see Grammar 9.3) to give;* dá-lhe
   jeito? *does it suit you?,* dá-me jeito *it
   suits me*
datar (de) *to date (from)*
deixar *to leave*
demorar *to delay, take a long time*
depois (de) *after*
desculpar *to excuse;* desculpe *I'm sorry*
desde *from, since*
desejar *to want, desire*
devagar *slowly*
deve *you should*
dever *to have to, to be obliged to*
Dezembro *December*
o dia *day*
o dinheiro *money*
o director, a directora *the director*
direito/a *right;* à direita *to the right*
disponível *free, available*
dizer *(see Grammar 9.3) to say*
a dobrada *tripe*
doce *sweet*
o doce *dessert, sweet;* o doce de
   laranja *orange preserve, marmalade*
o dólar *dollar*
doméstico/a *domestic, internal (flight)*
o domingo *Sunday*
donde *from where, whence*
a dose *helping;* meia dose *half portion*
dto. *(abbreviation, see* direito*)*
Dublim *Dublin*
duplo/a *double*
durante *during*
uma dúzia *a dozen*

E

e *and*
Edimburgo *Edinburgh*
o eléctrico *tram*
a ementa *menu*

o empregado, a empregada *employee*

o emprego *job, employment*

empurrar *to push*

encarnado/a *red*

encontrar *to meet*

o encontro *appointment*

o engenheiro *engineer*

então *then*

a entrada *entrance*

entrar *to enter, go in*

entre *between*

entregar *to hand over*

entretanto *meanwhile*

escocês/esa *Scottish*

Escócia *Scotland*

a escola *school*

o escudo *the basic unit of Portuguese currency*

escuro/a *dark*

a espécie *kind, type*

a espera *wait;* à espera de *waiting for;*
à minha espera *waiting for me*

esperar *to wait*

a espetada *kebab*

esq. *(abbreviation, see* esquerdo*)*

esquerdo/a *left;* à esquerda *to the left*

a esquina *corner*

esse, essa *that, that one*

a estação *station; season*

a estadia *stay;* boa estadia *have a good stay*

estar *(see Part I, Unit 4, 3; Part II, text 2
note 1 and text 3 note 2; Grammar
9.3) to be*

este, esta *this, this one*

o estilo *style*

a estrada *road*

exactamente *exactly*

exacto *exact*

experimentar *to try on*

F

falar *to speak;* fala... *this is... speaking*

faltar *to be lacking;* faltam dez
minutos *you have ten minutes / there are
ten minutes to go*

a farmácia *chemist's*

o fato *suit*

o favor *favour;* (se) faz favor *please;* por
favor *please*

faz *(see* fazer*)*

fazer *(see Grammar 9.3) to do, to make*

as febras *(pl.)* de porco *lean pork*

fechado/a *closed*

fechar *to shut, close*

a feijoada *bean stew*

a feira *fair*

o feriado *a public holiday, bank holiday*

as férias *(pl.) holidays;* estar de férias *to be on
holiday*

a festa *party*

Fevereiro *February*

o fiambre *cold ham*

ficar *(see Part I, Unit 4,5) to stay; to be;*
fica-lhe bem *it suits you / her / him*

o filete *fillet*

o fim *the end;* no fim de *at the end of*

a fome *hunger;* estar com fome *to be hungry*

a fonte *fountain*

o frango *chicken*

o frasco *pot, jar*

a frente *front;* em frente *ahead;* em frente
(de) *opposite, facing*

fresco/a *cool, fresh*

o frigorífico *refrigerator*

frito/a *fried*

a fruta *fruit*

a frutaria *fruit shop*

funcionar *to work, function;* não
funciona *it doesn't work*

o funcionário *official, clerk, civil servant*

o fundo *the bottom;* ao fundo de *at the
bottom of*

G

o galão *coffee with a lot of milk, served in
a glass*

galês/esa *Welsh*

a galinha *hen*

a garagem *garage*

o garoto *small white coffee*

a garrafa *bottle*

o gás *gas*

geralmente *generally*

a ginástica *gymnastics*

gostar (de) *to like*

o grama *gram weight*

grande *large, big*

grelhado/a *grilled*

o guia *guide book*

191

H

há… *there is / are;* há…? *is / are there…?*

haver *(see Grammar 9.3) to have (auxiliary verb)*

hoje *today;* hoje de manhã *this morning;* hoje à tarde *this afternoon;* hoje à noite *tonight*

o homem *man*

a hora *hour;* a que horas…? *at what time…?* a hora de ponta *rush hour*

o hotel *hotel*

I

a ida *outward journey;* um bilhete de ida e volta *return ticket*

a igreja *church*

impedido *engaged (telephone)*

uma imperial *a draught beer*

importante *important*

importar-se *to mind;* não se importa de…? *would you mind…?*

a impressão *impression*

a indicação *sign*

o indicativo *area code (for telephones)*

Inglaterra *England*

inglês / esa *English*

o ingrediente *ingredient*

interessante *interesting*

internacional *international*

o Inverno *winter*

ir *(see Grammar 9.3) to go*

Irlanda *Ireland*

irlandês / esa *Irish*

a irmã *sister*

o irmão (irmãos) *brother*

isso *that*

isto *this*

J

já *already;* até já *see you shortly;* já não há *there's none left*

Janeiro *January*

a janela *window*

jantar *to have dinner, to dine*

o jardim *garden*

a jardineira *meat and (finely chopped) vegetable stew*

o jarro *jug*

o jeito *(see* dar*)*

o jornal *newspaper*

o / a jornalista *journalist*

Julho *July*

Junho *June*

junto / a *beside*

L

lá *there*

a lã *wool*

o lado *side;* do lado esquerdo / direito (de) *on the left / right of;* ao lado (de) *beside, next to*

lamentar *to regret*

lamento *I'm sorry*

lanchar *to have an afternoon snack*

o lanche *afternoon snack*

o lápis *pencil*

a laranja *orange*

o largo *village, town or city square*

a lata *tin*

o leite *milk*

o lençol *sheet*

ler *(see Grammar 9.3) to read*

levantar-se *to get up*

levar *to take*

a libra *pound*

a licença *permission;* com licença *excuse me*

o licor *liqueur*

ligar *to connect*

o limão *lemon*

lindo / a *pretty, lovely*

o linguado *Dover sole*

a linha *line, telephone line*

o linho *linen*

Lisboa *Lisbon*

a lista *list, menu*

a lista telefónica *telephone directory*

o litro *litre*

a livraria *bookshop*

livre *free, vacant*

logo *immediately;* até logo *see you later*

a loja *shop*

o / a lojista *shopkeeper*

Londres *London*

longe *far away*

a louça *dishes, chinaware*

a lula *squid*

a luz *light*

M

a maçã *apple*
Maio *May*
maior *bigger;* é maior do que… *it is bigger than…;* o / a maior *the biggest*
mais *more*
o mal *harm;* não faz mal *it doesn't matter*
mal *badly*
a mala *suitcase*
a manhã *morning;* hoje de manhã *this morning*
a manteiga *butter*
a mão (mãos) *hand*
marcar o número *to dial the number;* marcar um encontro *to make an appointment*
o marido *husband*
o marisco *seafood*
a marmelada *quince preserve*
o mapa *map*
mas *but*
meio / a *half;* meio-dia *midday;* meia-noite *midnight*
o meio *middle;* no meio de *in the middle of*
o mel *honey*
o melão *melon*
melhor *better;* é melhor do que… *it is better than…;* o / a melhor *the best*
menos *less;* duas menos um quarto *a quarter to two*
o mercado *market*
a mercearia *grocer's*
o merceeiro *grocer*
o mês *month*
a mesa *table*
mesmo *even*
mesmo / a *same*
o metro *the underground railway; metre*
o meu, a minha *my, mine*
misto / a *mixed*
moçambicano / a *Mozambican*
a moda *fashion;* … à moda de… *…cooked in the… style*
o modelo *model*
um momento *one moment, please wait a moment*
a morada *residence, address*
morar *to live (in a place)*
muito *very;* muito prazer *pleased to meet you*

muitos / as *many*
a mulher *woman*
a música *music*

N

nada *nothing*
não *no*
a nata *cream*
natural *at room temperature*
a noite *night;* hoje à noite *tonight;* boa noite *good evening, good night*
o nome *name*
normalmente *normally*
o nosso, a nossa *our*
Novembro *November*
o número *size;* o número acima *the next size up*

O

o *the; him, it (pronoun)*
obrigado / a *thank you*
ocupado / a *engaged, occupied*
olá *hello*
o oleiro *potter*
o óleo *cooking oil; lubricating oil*
olhar *to look at;* olhe *look*
a omeleta *omelette*
onde *where*
ontem *yesterday*
óptimo / a *splendid, very good*
ora bem *well now*
ou *or*
ouço *(see ouvir)*
o ouro *gold*
o Outono *autumn*
outro / a *another*
Outubro *October*
ouvir* *(pres: ouço, ouves, ouve, ouvimos, ouvis, ouvem)* *to hear;* prazer em ouvi-lo / la *a pleasure to speak to you*
o ovo *egg*

P

o pacote *packet*
a padaria *bakery, bread shop*
o paio *Portuguese cured sausage*
o país *country (national territory)*
o pão (pães) *bread, loaf (loaves)*
a papelaria *stationer's*

para *for, to* (*e.g.* um bilhete para Lisboa)
o parque *park*
a partida *departure*
  partir *to leave, depart;* a partir
    das… *from… o'clock onwards*
o passaporte *passport*
  passear* (*pres:* passeio, passeias, passeia,
    passeamos, passeais, passeiam) *to go for
    a walk, to go on an excursion*
o pastel *pastry, cake*
a pastelaria *pastry shop, café*
o pé *foot;* a pé *on foot*
  peço (*see* pedir)
  pedir* (*pres:* peço, pedes, pede, pedimos,
    pedis, pedem) *to ask for;* pedir
    desculpa *to beg pardon;* peço desculpa
    I do beg your pardon; peço imensa
    desculpa *I'm terribly sorry*
a peixaria *fishmonger's*
o peixe *fish*
a pensão *guest house, small hotel*
  pequeno / a *small*
o pequeno almoço *breakfast*
  perceber *to understand*
  perfeito / a *perfect*
a pergunta *question*
  perguntar *to ask*
  perto *near*
a pescada *hake*
o pêssego *peach*
a pessoa *person*
  pior *worse;* é pior do que… *it is worse
    than…;* o / a pior *the worst*
a planta *plan (of city)*
  poder (*see Grammar 9.3*) *to be able*
a poluição *pollution*
o polvo *octopus*
a ponte *bridge*
  pôr (*see Grammar 9.3*) *to put*
  por *by, for, through*
  por exemplo *for example*
o porco *pork, pig*
  porque *because*
  porque…? *why…?;* porquê? *why?*
  portanto *so, consequently, therefore*
o porto *harbour;* o Porto *Oporto;* o vinho
    do Porto *port wine*
  português / esa *Portuguese*
  posso (*see* poder) *I may, can*
194 o postal *post card*

pouco *little, not much;* um pouco *a little*
a praça *square (in a village, town or city)*
a prata *silver*
o prato *dish*
o prazer *pleasure;* muito prazer *pleased to
    meet you;* prazer em ouvi-lo / la *(when
    phoning) nice to speak to you*
  precisar *to need*
o preço *price*
a preferência *preference*
  preferir* (*pres:* prefiro, preferes, prefere,
    preferimos, preferis, preferem) *to prefer*
  prefiro (*see* preferir)
  preocupar-se *to worry;* não se
    preocupe *don't worry*
o presunto *Parma-type cured ham*
a Primavera *spring*
  privativo / a *private, individual*
o problema *problem*
o produto *product*
o / a professor / a *teacher*
o programa *programme*
  provar *to try on*
  próximo / a *next, near;* o / a mais
    próximo / a *the nearest;* até
    à próxima *until the next time we meet*
o pudim *pudding;* o pudim flan *caramel
    custard*
  puxar *to pull*

Q

  qual…? quais…? *which…?*
a qualidade *quality*
  quando *when*
  quantos / as? *how many?*
a quarta-feira *Wednesday*
  quarto / a *fourth*
o quarto *room*
  quase *almost*
  que *that, which*
o queijo *cheese*
  quem *who, whom*
  querer (*see Grammar 9.3*) *to want*
o quilo *kilogram weight*
a quinta-feira *Thursday*
  quinto *fifth*

R

a razão *reason;* ter razão *to be right*